Exeter Civic Society 1989

West of the River

by Hazel Harvey

Front cover: *Georgian Houses in Okehampton Street,*
drawn by P. V. Pitman

Back cover: *Harvesting pinks below Hambeer Lane*

CW00546986

Foreword

This is the sixth in the series of
ance and history of the subu
completes the circle. Perhaps
to produce a booklet on Exeter

The series has brought great credit to the Civic Society and I must praise in particular Mrs Hazel Harvey, not only for researching and writing this particular booklet as well as those on Pennsylvania and Sidwell Street but also for her skill and hard work in the more mundane aspects of publication and distribution — she is an excellent saleswoman!

I have lived in Exeter since 1922 but always East of the River Exe, and before the War my memories of St Thomas and Exwick were of a somewhat run-down area, even "the Wild West"; since the War we have seen those parishes become increasingly suburban in nature with houses creeping up the green hills, always in spite of the Civic Society's protests. We hope that the tops of the hills will now be saved — our Planners mean well but too many appeals seem to be successful.

With these changes over the years, particularly the last twenty, it is important to realise that St Thomas and Exwick, particularly St Thomas, have a very considerable history of their own. I particularly commend this booklet so that Exonians, let alone visitors, may appreciate that there is a great deal to be discovered about Exeter West of the river other than suburban houses and shopping centres, however necessary those may be to modern life.

W. J. Hallett
Chairman, Exeter Civic Society

Exeter is cut off from its western suburbs by the wide river. Today we see the water as an obstacle to traffic, or a centre for leisure activities. For centuries the opposite was true: the river itself was the main thoroughfare, and its banks throbbed with industry. The Exe was the valley's major resource, but also a great threat, regularly flooding over the whole low-lying area.

It was the river that originally hollowed out the valley floor that St Thomas stands on. It was the river that caused Exeter to grow at this particular junction of cliff and crossing. Until the Middle Ages, sea-tides came to the quay, and when they ebbed one could wade across, or urge a horse through the shallow water. Ships could unload, and travellers could pass to west and east.

The river runs along one side of its flood-plain, leaving a wide flat valley to the west. Flat ground is in short supply in Exeter. Over the centuries, every activity, industry or sport that needs elbow-room has found it west of the river: space to dye cloth and hang it to dry, space for iron-foundries, plant-nurseries, wrestling, the Easter Fair, factories, the gasworks, the cattle-market, a railway — and houses for the railwaymen — an industrial estate, Park-and-Ride, and even in-town "out-of-town" supermarkets and sports centres.

Behind the level plain the ground rises, with tilted green fields like the sides of a jade bowl. Housing estates are steadily covering the bowl's pattern of hedges and pasture, but a green band can still be seen near the rim. A walk in the ridge-top lanes along this rim provides superb views: across the valley to the city crowned by cathedral and castle; and down the steep outside of the "bowl" on to a lumpy "cloth" of dumpy green hills.

Three main routes converge at Exe Bridges. The same choice faced the earliest west-bound pedlar or pilgrim as faces today's juggernauts and jams: left, right, or straight on? South beside the river; south-west along Cowick Street, taking the hills head-on as the old foot-folk always did; or north-west along Okehampton Street? The name Cowick is usually explained as Saxon for cow-farm, plausibly enough if nearby Cowley were also explained from *cow*, whereas that is said to be "Cufa's clearing." It is tempting to see in *Coic* (the earliest recorded form of *Cowick*) the survival of a local Latin name for the distinctive local feature; just as Coblenz is still named from the Latin for the confluence of Rhine and Moselle, might *Coic* not preserve the Latin *coicio*, "convergence of routes"?

There were Roman-Britons in Exeter for about 350 years. They may have dug the first leats that drained and divided Exe Island, Shilhay and Bonhay; and they may already have set mill-wheels in the leats. They probably either bridged or paved the ford across the main stream. Whether they crossed by bridge, ferry or ford, the starting-point was Shilhay. Many Roman coins have been found there, showing either that travellers threw a coin into the water for luck, or that many accidentally dropped their payment. (The modern equivalent is the scattering of coins near bus-stops, a welcome subsidy for cyclists.)

The western bank was low-lying and marshy. Alphington Road runs on a causeway for part of its length; and the section of Cowick Street from the railway-bridge to Old Vicarage Road may owe its straightness to origin as a Roman causeway. The straight section ends precisely at the point reached by the floods in, for example, 1800 and 1810. As the ground rises,

View from Little John's Cross. Pencil drawing in Devon & Exeter Institution.

Cowick Street begins to twist and turn. Buddle Lane and Cowick Lane stand noticeably higher, on a lip of ground above the flood-plain. *Buddle* may come from the Anglo-Saxon for "house", *bothl*; this is where a house could safely stand.

Over the centuries the marshes were drained, the slopes cleared, and farmhouses built. The local Roman-Britons may have begun the labour; from the end of the 7th century it may have been Saxon incomers who caught the river-salmon, grazed sheep on the salt-marshes, drove ox-ploughs across the gentler slopes, and let pigs rootle under the hill-top trees. By mid-10th century the West Saxons were certainly well-established in Devon, and had divided the shire into administrative districts called "Hundreds." The Hundred of Wonford covered a large dumb-bell-shaped area of which our lands formed the "waist," squeezed between Crediton and Exminster, while Wonford itself lay in the eastern bulge, and the western end was close to Okehampton.

According to Domesday, before the Conquest the manor of "Coic" was held by a Saxon called Ailmar, with land that eight ploughs could till. There were 8 villeins (small-holders), 3 bordars (smaller holders), 2 serfs, 1 rouncey (small horse), 3 beasts (oxen for the ploughs), 40 sheep (no cows mentioned!), one mill, 3 acres of woodland and 3 acres of meadow. "Essoic" (Exwick) was held by Eureuuacus (Earwaker) and likewise had 8 ploughs; there were 9 villeins, 5 serfs, 40 sheep, a mill, 3 acres of meadow, 50 acres of pasture and 3 acres of coppice. Between Buddle Lane and the river lay "Haia" (Hayes) held by Edric, next to "Sotrebroc" (Southbrook) held by Aluiet.

At the Battle of Hastings, one of William's generals was his nephew-by-marriage, Baldwin of Brionne. Baldwin was made Sheriff of Devon, entrusted with the construction and care of castles at Rougemont and Okehampton, and made lord of 159 manors in Devon, including Cowick and Exwick. Baldwin's home in Normandy was near the famous Benedictine abbey of Bec (yes, you *have* heard of it; their London property is still called Tooting Bec. And it was a prior of Bec, Lanfranc, who became the first Norman archbishop of Canterbury, and Anselm made the same career-move in 1093.) Baldwin's father had helped to found Bec, and when Baldwin's son inherited the family lands and obligations on both sides of the Channel, he made a gift to the French abbey of two of his English estates, Cowick and Exwick. This must have been between 1090 (when Baldwin died) and 1107 (when the son died.)

We know the names of some Cowick people around 1090 - 1100, because the Exeter Book and Leofric's Missal carry records of serfs being sold or freed at the "Hundred" court there. Regenere bought Alfrith from Regenolde the monk of Cowick. Edith, daughter of Leofric Locc (Lock), bought the freedom of herself and her children. Godwin Blaca (Black) bought himself, his wife and offspring from William Hosethe. The witnesses representing Cowick included Edmaer the priest, Alfric Hals and Agilword Pudding. There is even mention of a Sewin Pinca, surely an early Cowick Pince.

Bec set up a small daughter-priory in Cowick. "Priory Ruins" are marked in Flowerpot field in some maps, but it is more likely that the little community took over Cowick Barton farmhouse, and the Saxon burial-ground next to it, and gradually added cells, cloisters and church. William Warelwast (bishop of Exeter 1107-36, himself a Norman, indeed another nephew of the Conqueror) helped Cowick's building-fund by promising 60 days off purgatory for visiting the relics there. The cathedral's collection of relics included a piece of St Andrew's staff. Did Warelwast lend this to the new priory, giving it a dedication? Visitors to St Andrew's will have had a good view across to the bishop's rival enterprise, the construction of the Norman cathedral.

Two recent booklets tell the 400-year history of the priory: *In Search of Cowick* by Jean Awdas, and *The Monks of Cowick* by Geoffrey Yeo. The priory church was functioning by 1150. The monks also built guest-rooms for travellers and pilgrims, a bake-house to provide bread for the poor, a Great Grange to store the produce of the two manors and (with no neighbours to complain to the planning department) a Great Porch. One monk called Walter (possibly a prior of that name in the 1180s) had a vision of the terrors of purgatory, put on a hair-shirt, and was revered after his death as St Walter, attracting crowds of pilgrims on his name-day even 300 years later. Many little Exonians were named after him.

There was another small monastic building not far away, at Marsh Barton: St Mary of the Marsh, built by Plympton Priory for monks visiting Exeter. It had its own water-mill.

There were chapels at each end of Exe Bridge, still only a narrow footbridge made of "clappers of tymbre." (Bulky traffic or impoverished travellers used the ford alongside.) The chapel at the city end was dedicated to St Edmund, as Saxon chapels on bridges often were, since the king once escaped from the Danes by hiding under a bridge. The chapel at the western end was dedicated to Thomas à Becket. He was murdered and canonised in the 1170s, so the chapel may have dated from then, or an existing chapel may have been renamed to annoy Bishop Bartholomew, an enemy of Becket. If so, this was not the only time that space was found just across the river for something forbidden within the city walls.

Over the centuries, more and more industries came to the river-banks to exploit the water-supply, free power and shipment facilities. The mills at Exwick and Cowick had been grinding grain since Saxon times. In 1189 the priory bought 2 acres of river-meadow from Duryard to build a new weir for Exwick leat. Cowick mill drew its water off the end of the bridge-weir. Merchants and tradesmen built dwellings, workshops and warehouses on Exe Island and along the approach-roads to the bridge. There were soon enough residents in Cowick to call it a township. Tanners, brewers, metal-workers, cloth-makers and dyers plied their smelly trades. The leats around Exe Island alone were driving at least nine mills. The weavers began to produce more cloth than could be cleansed and felted by trampling on it in cold water, and carried it to be pounded mechanically in "tucking" or "fulling" mills.

A manor-house stood on each estate. One at Barley is mentioned in 1189. Randolf de Haga (1125) may have occupied the house on Hayes that preceded one fortified in the Civil War. The neighbouring estate, Southbrook, was beginning to be called Floyerhayes. It was handed down through many generations of the Floyer family (along with a silver bowl, since the estate carried the obligation that whenever the Earl of Devon set foot on Exe Island, his tenant had to stop whatever he might be doing and quickly step forward "decently apparelled with a fair sweet towel on his shoulder, a flagon of wine in one hand, and a silver bowl in the other, and offer to serve his lordship with drink.")

For many generations the lord enjoying this roadside service-station will have been a Courtenay. The Courtenays came to England with Eleanor of Aquitaine. They married into the Redvers family and into other branches of the Brionne family, gaining within 200 years control of the greater part of Devon, including most of the Exe Valley. Exeter's own jurisdiction did not extend one inch outside the city walls. The Courtenays controlled the river-banks, including the area between Bartholomew Street and the river, and the river itself. Indeed our own Earl wrote in 1966: "I think I am the only non-royalty who owns part of the river-bed."

In 1180 Robert de Courtenay was the lord of Exe Island. He granted to Nicholas Gervase "all his water which Thomas the Fuller holds outside the West Gate between the corn-mills and Crickenpette." Gervase was a prominent citizen who owned mills and warehouses near the bridge. He saw many travellers drown on the ford, and the wooden bridge swaying in the winter floods. He determined to rebuild the bridge in stone, and dispatched his son (Walter!) to collect donations from near and far. It took many decades at the turn of the 13th century to complete the work. The bridge had to be about 700 feet long, crossing not only the stream but also the salt-marshes. Half still stands, enjoying a peaceful retirement in the drained marshes between Frog Street and Edmund Street.

Drawings of this bridge done in the 1660s and 1760s show the central pier with a door at water-level, leading to a "Pixy House." This has been explained as yet another chapel, housing a sacred *pyx*; or a *pixhay*, a fairy house, a public urinal; or was it something *piscatorial*, a place to spear salmon as they leapt upstream? Three 17th-century travellers mentioned the fishing. Risdon wrote in 1605: "The River Ex (is) well stored with salmon; which are reputed the best in this land, for at most times you shall find some come new from the sea with lice on their backs, and then they are best." A lieutenant from Norwich in 1635 saw "…. a faire stone Bridge of 20 arches, under w[ch] the dainty Salmon Trouts come trolling." Celia Fiennes in 1695 recorded that "they catch the salmon as they leap, with spears."

Back to when the bridge was young: in the 1240s a devout woman settled on it as a hermit, blocking the traffic for more than five years while the city tried to formulate a bye-law against squatting; or was it a parking offence, or possibly drinking in a public place? The obstruction must have inconvenienced many, including the Cowick monks (who at this time were all Frenchmen, sent over from Bec, who wore white undyed wool, not monastic black.)

Soon after 1250 the bridge-chapels were upgraded to parish churches. Bishop (Walter!) Bronescombe installed John as rector of St Edmund's in 1259, and Henry as vicar of St Thomas in 1261. Cowick Priory provided stipend and manse for Henry, and the little flood-damaged chapel was rebuilt in stone. (An archway from this building is preserved in the north porch of the present parish church.) As the river-bank could not be used for a graveyard, the parishioners continued to bury their dead next to the Priory. A small cemetery chapel, St Michael's, was built there in the 1270s.

A grander project dominated the view of the city. Bishop Bronescombe was rebuilding the entire nave of the cathedral. An immense amount of stone was needed. One of the quarries listed in the fabric rolls for 1324/5 is Barley. An inventory of the Priory's possessions from the same year enables us to picture cartloads of stone trundling down Dunsford Road past fields of barley and of rye, oats, wheat, beans and peas. The Priory's livestock that year amounted to 4 horses, 11 oxen, 116 sheep, 41 pigs and 3 peafowl (still no cows; cheese was made from ewes' milk). The monks had 24 free tenants and 10 unfree.

Their Courtenay overlords had inherited the obligations of their original patron. When Sir Hugh died near Colyton in 1291, he was brought to the Priory for burial. A stone coffin

OLD EXE BRIDGE
South Side

Old Exe Bridge. Drawing in Devon & Exeter Institution.

and a lead chalice were found on the site in 1887. The coffin may well have been Sir Hugh's. (It is on display at present in St Nicholas' crypt.) In 1328 Sir Hugh's widow died in London and was brought to Cowick to lie next to him. Their son, another Hugh, and his wife, who died shortly before him in 1340, were also interred at Cowick. This Hugh had revived the title of earl in 1335, and the present numbering of the Earls of Devon starts with him.

He it was who in 1311 had blocked the gap in Countess Isabella's weirs, preventing ships and salt water from reaching Exeter Quay. His elaborate funeral took up a long weekend. On the Friday, virtually all of Devon's nobility, gentry and top clergy escorted the coffin from Tiverton to Exeter; it lay in the cathedral for solemn vespers and a mass; the procession re-assembled on the Monday and walked to Cowick, where Bishop Grandisson presided over the interment in the choir. A tile-floor patterned with the Courtenay arms may date from then. Hugh's successor died in 1375 and was buried in the cathedral, but he had remembered Cowick in his will: "Jeo devise a la meson de Couwyk cent soulds." In 1376 William Courtenay, Bishop of London, ordained 99 clerics at Cowick, including yet another Hugh Courtenay.

In 1384 a torrential flood burst the river-banks, demolished part of the bridge, and swept away the foundations of St Thomas' Chapel. The Priory decided to rebuild on a new site, well away from the river, nearer to the centre of the parish. Land on Cowick Street (still occupied by the present church and its spacious churchyard) was granted by Prior de Bourgeanyll to John Floyer and one Holland (churchwardens) and John Alkebarne (vicar). The field was called Pyryhay, perhaps from Adam de Piris, prior in 1289. The new church was consecrated on 4th October 1412, and the churchyard on the following day. St Michael's cemetery was used only occasionally thereafter, and not at all after 1729.

John Holland, Duke of Exeter, had a fine mansion in Cowick Street just east of the church. Richard Holland built the mansion at Bowhill by 1429 (Bishop Lacey licensed a private chapel on 28th April). In the 1460s Thomas Horsey and Nicholas Stocker leased fields west of Cowick Lane.

While parish, town and gentry flourished, the Priory declined. It forfeited all its income when England was fighting France in the 1420s. Numbers dwindled to prior and one monk, with no funds to repair the priory or its possessions. A disastrous fire on Palm Sunday 1442 damaged what remained. The small community struggled on until 1451, then withdrew to Bec. The estates passed to Eton College, then in 1462 to Tavistock Abbey, which sent English monks to the Priory. They set up a fulling-mill and cloth-racks in Cowick, and re-established the "good life" in both senses — regular prayer and efficient farm-management.

In 1497 Perkin Warbeck and his army marched through St Thomas, encircled the city and tried to force an entry.

1539 was a year of even greater disturbances and new beginnings. The Courtenays had fallen from grace and lost control of the Exe valley. In 1539 Henry VIII agreed that access should be restored to Exeter Quay; this launched the idea of England's first ship-canal. Also in 1539 Lord John Russell was sent to supervise the change-over to the New Religion and the closure of the monasteries. In return he was granted many of the great monastic estates, including Tavistock and therefore Cowick and Exwick. He had Cowick Priory demolished, along with St Walter's shrine, and a fine new mansion built. Cowick Barton still stands, now a pub, its sign boasting 1657 from the date on one chimney-piece. In fact the house is older, probably pre-1547, from the evidence of a window (now in the Victoria & Albert Museum) which shows the arms of Russell's ward, the future Edward VI.

In 1546 the vacated monastic building at Marsh Barton was granted to James Coffin and Thomas Godwin. They converted it to a mansion called simply "Marsh," and eventually sold to James Buller. Hayes, which, as a prebend, had helped maintain the castle chapel, was purchased by a prominent city merchant called Peter (or Petre). Between 1560 and 1590 he built a new manor-house there, with a walled yard.

The vicar of St Thomas during these changes was a Cornishman, Robert Welshe, appointed by Tavistock in 1537 and retained by Russell in 1539. When Henry VIII frowned on dedications to Becket, Welshe shortened the church's name to plain "St Thomas" which could mean the martyr, or the apostle.

In 1542 plague swept through the parish, killing 106 in a population of 500 to 700.

Whitsunday 1549 was the deadline for the change from Latin masses and Roman vestments to services according to the new English Book of Common Prayer. Cornishmen, passionate to retain the old rites, marched into England, gathering support as they came. When they reached St Thomas, they outnumbered the citizens of Exeter, who barred the gates against them. Robert Welshe tried to control the rebels during the subsequent siege. His contemporary, John Hooker, portrays him as a straightforward, sportsmanlike, unfoppish man: he was "of no great stature, but well sett and mightelie compacte he was a verie good wrasteler, shott well, bothe in the longe bowe as also in the crosse bowe, he handeled his handgonne and pece verie well he was... suche a one as wolde not geve his hed for

the pollinge nor his bearde for the washeinge..."

There were violent incidents during the five-week siege, and bloody clashes in the surrounding countryside. One of Lord Russell's messengers was captured, tried by the mob, and hanged from an elm tree on Exe Island. A belligerent gunman wanted to burn down the city by firing red-hot shot into the streets. Welshe dissuaded him; this saved the city, but did not save the vicar from being condemned as a ringleader of the rebellion, a traitor. Treason is a political crime, but his execution was played out as a gruesome spectacle which made it only too clear that the quarrel was about religious practices. Welshe was hauled to the top of his own church-tower, in his "Romish vestments," and the Old Religion was hanged there with him in the shape of "a holye water bucket, a sprinkle, a sacringe bell, a payre of beddes and such other lyke popyshe trashe..." His corpse was tarred and left dangling on the tower-roof until Mary came to the throne — four years later.

The city was rewarded for standing firm against the rebels; it was granted the manor of Exe Island, which still included land on both sides of the river.

Work went ahead on England's first ship-canal. William Floyre of Floyrehays transferred to the city in 1567, in language that conveys the great muddy mess made by the workmen, "All that ground, soil & terrytory as well now digged trenched & caste up for a new water course... digged, banked, moyned, trenched wrought, levyed & cast up or measured out, for & towards the better bryngyng, carrying, & recarrying of Botes & vessels with Wares & merchandices or other things from the High sea... to a place beneathe Bole Poole called Old Exe."

Another part of Floyerhayes, the former mill-site, had been occupied since 1520 by the Birdall family, casting bronze

9

cauldrons and skillets where Sainsbury's now sells ingredients for woks and microwaves. In 1560 the Birdalls moved their long-established South Street iron-works there, and occasionally cast massive bells. In 1616 the cathedral decided "that John Birdall should new cast and make tuneable the bells in the South Tower." One dated 1617 is still in use and bears John's initials.

Around 1640, Barley and Franklyn (and many other estates in Cowick) changed hands. The Russells were liquidising all their assets to pour into their great Fen-draining project in East Anglia. The Goulds became major land-owners. William Gould had bought Cowick from the Russells, and Hayes from the Peters; he died in 1635 (leaving money for a school in St Thomas). William's brother, Henry Gould, owned Floyerhayes (and bought Lew Trenchard from General Monk's father). A Gould heiress married a James Buller in 1739. This is how the Lordship of the riverside manors passed from Baldwin to Courtenay to Russell to Gould to Buller.

The Civil War brought fire and destruction to the river-banks. The city was held alternately for the King and for Parliament. The opposing side occupied outlying houses, watching and waiting. The Royalists had fortified the most substantial buildings in Cowick Street, the church, the gaol and the West Indies Inn, and Hayes manor-house. On 31st July more than 1100 Roundheads sallied out over the bridge with muskets and cannon. They took more than 80 Royalist prisoners, and drove the others back to the higher ground. Excavations on Flowerpot in 1986 found little musket-balls and a 1 lb cannon-ball against the yard walls, and signs that the house had burnt down.

In 1644-5 wounded Royalists were nursed in "Cowack House." In January 1646 General Fairfax encircled Exeter, pressing close to the St Thomas stronghold. On 30th January the church had been burnt down, probably deliberately to prevent his making use of it. In early February he occupied Barley House. He went to fight in North Devon and Cornwall, but on 31st March he came back over Redhill and through Exwick and Cowley. That night the city surrendered, but no treaty was signed until the Royalists had ceded "Hunkses Fort" in St Thomas (probably the fortified prison).

The church was so badly damaged that it had to be completely demolished. The vicarage and church houses were "alsoe pulled down in the Warr time." A public appeal was launched in 1654, and the church was rebuilt in 1656-7. The new tower was taller. The dedication was explicitly to Thomas the apostle. Cromwell ruled. St Thomas had a Presbyterian minister until 1662, when John Reynolds (grand-father of the artist Joshua) was installed as an Anglican vicar. Houses were built in Cowick Street to replace those destroyed in the Civil War (and were themselves destroyed in 1959 and 1962 during road-widening).

Quakers had begun to hold private meetings in Exeter. They were arrested and imprisoned if discovered, having their property seized. When George Fox came to Exeter in 1657, he took care to lodge outside the city, and Friends from Plymouth, Land's End and elsewhere joined him "at the sign of the Seven Stars, an inn at the bridge foot," and they had a "blessed heavenly meeting." Fox continues: "Next morning Major Blackmore sent soldiers to apprehend me; but I was gone before they came. As I was riding up the street, I saw the officers going down. The soldiers examined some Friends after I was gone, 'what they did there'; but when they told them that they were in their inn, and had business in the city, they went away without meddling any further with them."

On Monday 5th November 1688 William of Orange landed at Brixham. His baggage-ships sailed on to Topsham, but his troops began the long overland plod towards Exeter, Oxford and London, through mud and drizzle. By the Thursday a bedraggled column was marching through St Thomas, so numerous that it took three hours to pass. On the Friday William himself rode through, with his guards, to enter the city by the West Gate. A printed pamphlet describes a splendid procession: "200 blacks, brought from the plantations of the Netherlands in America, having on embroidered caps lined with white fur, and plumes of white feathers, to attend the horse... 200 Finlanders in beaver skins, taken from beasts they had slain, with black armour, and broad flaming swords ... the Prince on a milk white palfrey, armed cap-a-pee, a plume of white feathers on his head, in bright armour, and forty-two footmen running by him." Army records tell a different tale; they list the many sick soldiers left behind in Exeter, but no blacks, who would surely have been affected by Devon damp.

The Exeter cloth merchants are said to have supplied dry outfits for some of the sodden rank and file. The cloth-trade was still flourishing, its manufacturing processes dominating the area round Exebridge — witness Dr William Stukeley in 1724: "The bridge over the Isca is of great length and has houses on both sides and both ends; a considerable void space in the middle; there is a church upon it with a tower steeple... Woollens are brought here to be dyed, which we saw in passing over the bridge amongst the suburbs, consisting of dye-houses and drying-frames, spread in crowds on the banks of the river."

Izacke's map of 1741 shows these serried racks on "Shilley" and all the river banks. For centuries the river-side must have seemed decked for a permanent festival, with the colourful lengths of dyed cloth stretched to dry on tenterhooks. The wool trade has left its mark on local surnames, the many present-day Tuckers, Woollacotts, Woolleys, Fullers and Dyers. Even Willey's engineering works developed from woollen mills on Shilhay. The family may have been running them since the days of descriptive surnames, since one of the processes which turns wool into yarn is called willeying.

In the 1720s Exeter would not license travelling players within the city, and once again the first inn beyond the bridge was the venue for something banned in the city. Performances took place in an upper room, or occasionally in the garden. In 1721 the citizens flocked over the bridge to see "Punch's theatre, with artificial actors, also many wonderful Fancies as dancing with swords by a girl but ten years old, who turns many 100 times round with so swift a motion that it's scarce possible to distinguish her Face from the hinder part of her Head." In 1726 the Duke of Grafton's company of comedians advertised "a Diverting Comedy, called *The Busie Body*, at the Seven Stars at the Bridge foot in St Thomas."

John Gay's *Beggars' Opera* opened in London in January 1728. The original company gave the last performance of the season on 15th November at the Seven Stars, "and before the Play, at the earnest Request of divers of the Gentry, Mr Radford will perform his Agility, which is the last time he proposes ever to do it in Publick." The Seven Stars continued to serve as Exeter's oldest theatre even when proper stages were opened in the city.

In 1754 an attempt to mine coal on Exwick Hill, on the Cleave estate, was abandoned when the drill broke on a sledgehammer-head thrown in by a saboteur. The only other coal-mining venture in this county was in North Devon.

Obelisk "Erected by Northmore at Cleave after he lost Election — with inscription it closed for ever a Coal Field." — Drawing in Devon & Exeter Institution

In 1769 the Exeter Turnpike Act authorised a new Exe Bridge. The marshes had been drained and built on, the river was narrower and deeper, and the new bridge could be shorter. However, a public meeting in 1773 protested that the new design was "extravagant in its dimensions, of partial use, ill-chosen in site, a bridge that must prove a lasting subject of ridicule." It went ahead, and was nearly complete when a flood brought it down. The stones were recovered, a new architect was appointed, and "a handsome three-arch bridge" was completed in 1778. Halfway across, a stone marked the border between Exeter and the County of Devon. New Bridge

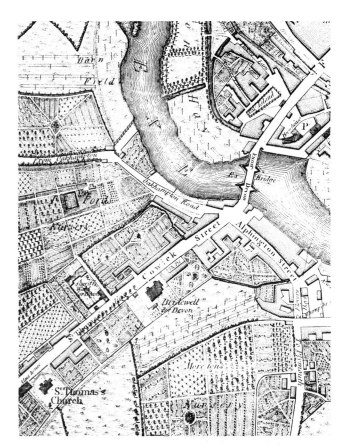

Charles Tozer's map, 1792

Street was constructed, in line with the new crossing. Gervase's bridge was demolished, except for the landward half, bearing St Edmund's Church and other buildings.

By now St Thomas had about 2000 inhabitants, some 300 families in "the town" (around the parish church and within the turnpikes), and 59 in scattered farmhouses. In 1806 Jenkins wrote "Were it not for its vicinity to Exeter this parish would appear as a large country town."

The St Thomas Hospital for Lunatics moved into Bowhill House on 1st July 1803. This stood below the Bowhill mansion, on the north-west corner of the crossroads, just outside the turnpike. The hospital's hope was cure rather than incarceration, by forbidding contact with razors, scissors, beer, sugar and tea. There were six "airing grounds" (three spacious walled courts and three gardens) and five indoor galleries. The inmates, some quite well-to-do, were encouraged to seek amusement, visit friends and take drives; and in the winter months, night and morning had their feet rubbed. By 1869 this caring establishment had proved so successful that it moved to grander accommodation at Wonford. The huge building was demolished. The bricks were used to build houses at Edgerton Park in Pennsylvania.

Bowhill House stood just above the flood-plain. On 9th November 1800 there had been "a prodigious flood; all the streets in St Thomas were inundated, the water reaching up to the windows." A boat was rowed up Cowick Street, dragged by horse-drawn sledge to Okehampton Street and re-launched. In January 1809 floods carried away the centre of Cowley Bridge, and all the tenter-racks on Bonhay and Shilhay. The following winter brought an even greater flood (greater even than the one in 1960). On 9th November 1810 the remaining arches of Cowley Bridge were washed away. Three large ships

Dunsford Tollgate, drawn by James Townsend. W.S.L.

Bowhill House. The 1803 asylum was enlarged in 1824 and 1848. Drawing in Devon & Exeter Institution

were thrown on to the Quay. St Thomas Vicarage had been rebuilt just after the floods of 1800-01 with its floor 3 inches higher. The 1810 flood rose just enough to meet the challenge.

In the same years that the river wrought such destruction, its power was being harnessed for more and more industrial development. For centuries the fulling mills and grist mills at Exwick had utilised the strong combined flow of Exe, Creedy and Culm. In the small peaceful settlement tucked in the creases between humpy green hills, Jenkins (1806) says that "Edmund Granger and Samuel Banfill have established a large woollen manufactory and erected spinning machines, workshops, dye-houses, tenter-grounds etc. Also dwelling-houses for the manufacturers." When these mills were advertised for sale in 1830, the description read: "Upon a very powerful stream of water, with a Factory, Fulling Mills, Gig Mills, Warehouse, Dye Houses, Drying Houses, Picking Shops, Spinning Rooms, Drying Lofts, Stabling, Weaving and Press Shops; 15 cottages and gardens for workmen."

Granger's main interest was his wine-business in the city, and the refurbishment of Rougemont House. Banfill, however, lived close to his work-force and their worries. His letters on the subject survive, as do the sturdy brick cottages he built.

1832 brought cholera to Exeter. One of the first cases reported was in St Thomas, which suffered a further 274 cases, only 38 ending in death. This unusual success-rate was credited to the prompt ministrations of the local doctor, and the healthy living conditions west of the river, where people were less crowded than in the city.

Exwick's population, both agricultural and manufacturing, was expanding fast. The hamlet was considered large enough, and far enough from the parish church, to require a chapel-of-

ease. The decisive factor may have been the vicar's enthusiasm for Pugin's Gothic revival. The Revd John Medley founded the Exeter Diocesan Architectural Society in 1841, the first of its kind outside Oxbridge. A new chapel could incorporate all the latest ideas about Christian socialism and the sacredness of pointed arches. Medley appointed a young architect, John Hayward (whose later career would provide such local landmarks as St Luke's College, the Royal Albert Memorial Museum, and New Blundell's.)

James Buller, lord of the manor and patron of the parish, donated £100 and the site, and on 30th July 1841 laid St Andrew's foundation stone. Medley expressed his joy that the equality of all in the eyes of God would be mirrored in the seating arrangements: open benches, all free, all of equal height. The builder was Moore, of St Thomas. The vicar asked the workmen not to desecrate their work by any profane swearing or immoral conduct. A bottle, containing a parchment scroll recording the event, and three small silver coins, was sealed inside the foundation stone. At 11 a.m. on Monday, 26th September 1842, the chapel was filled to over-flowing for the consecration. Afterwards, the bishop's party took lunch at Medley's house, and in a tent near the chapel 250 poor children from the St Thomas Schools "were regaled with roast beef and plum pudding through the kindness of the Revd J. Ford of Barley House."

In the middle decades of the 19th century, food prices were high in Exeter, and poor families were hungry and restless. There were food-riots in May 1847 and January 1854. In January 1855 it was so cold that the Exe froze (and Mr. Vickary roasted a joint of meat on the ice at the back of the Seven Stars Hotel). In November 1867 there was such unrest that the usual Cathedral Yard bonfire was cancelled, and the

Riot Act was read to the hungry crowd. The militia tried to hold the bridge with fixed bayonets, but the mob stormed into St Thomas to fetch the timber-wagons, and to attack food-shops and smash windows.

In such times it was as well to be self-sufficient. John Stocker described Cowick Street in the 1860s: there were "many thatched houses and any number of courts. The kitchens were floored with pebbles. Nearly all the houses had tiny gardens and nearly every cottage kept pigs. In Reed's Court there were 20 houses and about 100 pigs."

This almost medieval way of life continued in the shadow of the railway viaduct built across the town by the South Devon Railway. In August 1844 the directors had decided, on Brunel's advice, to adopt the Atmospheric System invented by Messrs Samuda Bros and Clegg. Their idea was to pull trains not with locomotives but by stationary steam-engines three miles apart in pumping-stations, that would create a vacuum in a pipe lying along the track. The train inserted a piston in a slit in the top of the pipe and — when all went well — sped along like a draper's cash-capsule, at up to 68 mph, smoothly, quietly and cleanly, with none of the smells, smuts or shudders of a steam locomotive.

By February 1845 the Samudas and Clegg had nearly completed a stone viaduct of 62 arches, almost a third of a mile long, across the centre of St Thomas. By Whitsun 1846 the line was laid as far as Teignmouth, but the atmospheric apparatus had not arrived; locomotives were used for the grand opening. The report in the *Flying Post* conveys the novelty of the experience: "On the beautiful banks of the Exe what a change has been wrought — scenery the most lovely that can be conceived of has been laid open to the view of thousands, many of whom though natives of this locality had not seen it before." At noon the first passenger train from St David's station "swept past the west and south faces of the City and suburbs with a velocity that set at nought that of the arrow."

On Whit Monday there were such crowds in Exeter wanting to see Teignmouth, and vice versa, that extra trains were laid on, and Teignmouth put out all the flags, "while from the bosom of old ocean came the echo of the joy and hilarity that reigned in the land."

In September 1847 the line began to be worked by the atmospheric system, but the expensive "caper" had to be abandoned, and in September 1848 the steam locomotives were brought back. The salt air of the estuary and coast was blamed for perishing the leather flaps which had to seal the slit along the vacuum pipes, but the system had also failed in Croydon in 1846, far from the sea. One pumping station survives, at Starcross.

Until St Thomas became "the railway town," the only built-up areas were along the three streets near the river. Now row upon row of terrace houses began to cover the nursery grounds between the main streets. The inhabitants could enjoy an ocean dip before work, for the price of a sixpenny return on the early Bathing Train to Dawlish.

In 1882 horse-drawn trams began a service to Alphington. The electric trams that replaced them in 1905 ran as far as Stone Lane on Alphington Road, and to the Falmouth Inn at the top of Cowick Street.

In the 1880s the population of St Thomas increased by one third, and by one fifth again in the 1890s. In 1899 it became part of the Exeter municipal area. A census on Exe Bridge showed that 3722 people crossed daily between 6 and 10 am,

The 1801 O.S. shows more fields than houses

THE LAST CAR TO DUNSFORD HILL

3753 between noon and 2 pm, and 5610 between 7 and 11 in the evening. On Saturdays the evening figure rose to 10,000. The city and its transiscan suburb were clearly mutually dependent for labour, employment, supplies, custom and entertainment. In 1904-5 a new single-span steel bridge was built, the first pin-bridge in England.

Alphington Street was widened to take the heavy traffic to the new electricity works, the canal, and Willey's. Okehampton Street remained too narrow for trams, and funerals often found hay-carts blocking the way to the cemetery. The countryside was still very near. Until the 1920s, Buddle Lane was still a narrow high-hedged Devon lane. A small girl used to wake there to a view of Barley House fields where "the shadows chased one another and the rabbits played, and we heard the rooks in the elms." Below the lane was a flowery meadow. "Long ago, the sight of that buttercup field made the mother of a friend decide to come and live near us... In summer I have been woken by cart-horses clip-clopping down our narrow back lane; horses called in to help with the hay-making had broken out of some nearby field and were taking a midnight stroll."

At the rear of the *Seven Stars*, the landlord and his chosen friends would fish for salmon from a boat. "Archie Lucas, architect to the city, had a special spot under the Seven Stars Inn where he used to fish. He kept all his casts in the basement. You could stand on the bridge and watch him pulling in the salmon. He used to pull some out of there, I can tell you."

The Seven Stars from the river, drawn by P. V. Pitman

In 1917 there was a severe frost, with skating under Exe Bridge. A bicycle was ridden from Cowley Bridge to the Fish Quay, and an ox was roasted on the ice.

Willey's was making aeroplane parts and shell cases for the war. For years Willey's was Exeter's largest employer. When the hooter went at knocking-off time, 1000 bikes would stream past the bridge.

The City Basin was fairly quiet in the 1920s, only three ships visiting regularly. A small tanker, the *Ben Jonson*, came from Southampton every month to fill BP's storage-tank. A Swedish ship supplied the large timber mill. Salt cod from Newfoundland was brought to a warehouse; this fish was tasty but generally known as "toe-rag."

In the second World War, Willey's employed 1300 (including 400+ women) making weapons and parts, possibly attracting Exeter's first air-raid, in August 1940, which damaged houses nearby. On the night of 23rd-24th April 1942, bombs fell on Okehampton Street, killing five. In the major raid on 3rd-4th May, the damage included the end house in Isca Road. Willey's lost its roofs, and work continued under 500 tarpaulins on the huge steel tanks for Mulberry Harbour. American forces mustered in the Cattle Market. Black GIs hung around the chip shop in Cowick Street in the evenings, the city being out of bounds.

After the war, council houses were built at Buddle Lane and Redhills, beginning the gradual spread of housing up the green slopes. Did they know something? In the 1960s came the famous floods. Many earlier ones have been mentioned. The parish registers for 1657 record 'a great ffloud," and 1659 "then another greater ffloud than that." There had also been serious flooding in 1894, 1917, 1920, 1929 and 1950.

Exe Bridge looking west, by P. V. Pitman

Cowick Street looking east

On 27th October 1960 42,000 tons of water per minute swept through the lower part of St Thomas, inundating 2500 houses, factories, churches and pubs. Another greater flood only 5½ weeks later strengthened the general feeling that drastic counter-measures were needed. For details of the flood-prevention schemes, see the Exwick Walk.

The 1905 bridge had obstructed the flood-waters. Study of a model established where to site new twin bridges. The new lay-out was also supposed to relieve the traffic-jams at the crossing. A start was made by demolishing the long-established shops and businesses that stood between the river and the railway. A "cat's cradle" of underpasses and loops was devised. Mayor Hallett opened Exe Bridge North on 30th July 1969 with a plaque-unveiling and a tea party, and Mayor Sargent its southern counterpart on 15th May 1972, with less junketing. The 1905 bridge was then demolished.

Gateway developed a shopping precinct west of the railway bridge, planned around the motor-car, with most of the area devoted to 100 parking-places. The Albany site stood derelict during many years of discussion, until finally a large supermarket and indoor-sports complex were built just where their car-borne customers would block the traffic as they left. As with all new road-schemes, such "unforeseen" increase in use soon brought it to a standstill. Exeter really does need to return to its excellent rail network. Let this be the lesson learned from St Thomas, the railway town.

We start at the corner of Haven Road (1 on map). Gervase Avenue commemorates the builder of the medieval stone bridge. Shooting Marsh Stile harks back to the days when the riverbank was fit only for fowling. In 1984, before this end of Haven Road was re-aligned, the city archaeological unit found evidence of centuries of industrial activity here: medieval mill-leat, then iron-working, brick-making as early as 1700, sugar-refining, horn-work, serge-making, tanning, and brewing.

What a contrast with the frivolous structure across the way, a "tropical lagoon" behind an undulating glass wall. The original plan for a serious sports centre with Olympic pool, possibly financed by incorporating a small pub or food-shop, has mutated to this light-hearted leisure-centre, providing exercise for motorised yuppies, and a water-chute and fun-food for their kids. A large part of the site went to Sainsbury's, and an even larger part to the currently favourite sport of parking. The Plaza was opened by the Princess of Wales on 2nd July 1986 (2 on map).

The Cycle Path crosses the Exe behind safety railings, and spirals down to the towpath. Things were different when 1,000 bikes would sweep along the road as Willey's hooter sounded.

The riverside is at last being developed. The old red-sandstone oast-houses (3 on map), from which the smell of malting barley drifted from the late 18th century until September 1949, are to be incorporated into a hotel, designed by a firm based in Swindon, Lovell Urban Renewal. The Haven Banks scheme, which will include houses, flats, restaurants, shops and a piazza, has already brought a design award to architects Halliday and Meecham even before it is built.

The elegant Cricklepit Footbridge (4 on map) was designed by David Hubbard and opened on 29th June 1988 by Mayor O'Callaghan; Montgomery School pupils processed in costumes from the times of previous bridges. When the hole was dug for the bridge-support, surprising new evidence for the age of Whipton stone was discovered — fossil spore 250 million years old.

The Maritime Museum (5 on map) was opened in 1969, and is run by ISCA (International Sailing Craft Association). Its fascinating and comprehensive collection of working boats from all over the world ranks second only to the Cathedral in Exeter's attractions. It has recently withdrawn from the Quay warehouses to the buildings round the canal basin. Previously the ferry crossing was part of the fun.

Visitors can also watch restoration work in the Boat Workshops in the former Electricity Generating Hall (façade designed by Donald Cameron, built 1903-05, closed down by the C.E.G.B. in 1960).

The Canal Basin, 900 feet long, 18 feet deep, was opened by the Mayor and Chamber on Michaelmas Day 1830. The canal was the first in England in the 1560s. It was modernised in 1827 by James Green. It escaped nationalisation in 1948 and is now run by Exeter's Quay and Canal Trust. A turntable from the branch railway built in 1867 now provides unusual seating.

The Exeter Sea Cadets have a handsome new H.Q. built from stone from Starcross Hospital and opened in December 1988 after they had lost their accommodation on the Quay. The Welcome Inn was built beside the canal late in the last century, with stone sash windows. Is there a connection with Welcome Street? The pub is lit with free gas supplied by its neighbour. Exeter pioneered the use of gaslight in the West Country. The

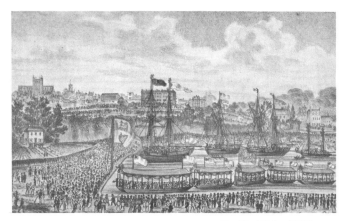

Opening the new Bason at Exeter, Sep^{tr.} 29th, 1830

Exeter Gas Light & Coke Company was set up in 1815 on Exe Island. A rival company chose a Haven Banks site in 1836. On 1st May 1839 the two companies merged, and in the 1870s the Exe Island works were shut down. In 1903 a tramway was built to bring coal from the basin. In Isca House (6 on map) the new offices of British Gas are long, low and elegant in their waterside meadow.

The Towpath offers a pleasant walk towards Double Locks and the Riverside Park.

Cotfield Street will bring us to Water Lane, where we turn right, past industrial buildings. Willey's engineering works (7 on map) shut down in 1980 after a long and proud history. Henry Frederick Willey had been bound apprentice in 1844 to William Canute Bodley. The name Bodley was then synonymous with kitchen-range, since Mr. George Bodley had patented in 1805 "a portable stove or kitchen for dressing victuals." H. F. Willey built up his own engineering firm to one of the largest in the west of England. In 1860 he moved it from Shilhay to Water Lane. He died in 1894, and his son Henry Alfred took over. He was a benevolent employer, believing in profit-sharing, workmen-directors, educational trips to America, a works' band, pensions, gardens and dwellings for his men, anything "which should make a straightforward workman's life a pleasure." He had one of the first motor-cars seen in Exeter, and would have liked to start a car factory. One of the many things Willey's did make was gas-meters, and when Stephen Simpson invented the coin-in-the-slot gas meter he was taken on as a director.

Next to Willey's on Tan Lane was another famous iron-foundry. The name Garton & King can be read on countless man-hole covers and pavement-gutters. The firm started in 1661 with a foundry in Waterbeer Street. In 1847 they made the radiators for the tropical house in Kew Gardens. They later incorporated Taylor & Bodley and made gear-wheels up to 9 ft. diameter, and aluminium bodies for ice-cream machines.

Isca Road, 1906-07, was Exeter's first council housing. Henry Willey had donated land nearby for a mission church for the new streets. It was built in 1904 and named after the old St Andrew's priory. It was of the same construction as the surviving St Philip's in Buddle Lane. In 1942 a tip-and-run daylight bomber hit the end of Isca Road, and the blast made the "tin" church sag and collapse, although the church hall survived and is now in commercial use. In 1945 the damaged houses in Isca Road were the first in Britain to be re-built under an apprenticeship scheme — see the stone on No. 2.

Well Park Brewery erected a sturdy building in red and yellow brick in the 1890s. Since the brewery stopped production in the 1960s it has been used as a furniture depository and is now a bathroom shop.

At the railway bridge Alphington Street becomes Alphington Road. It was called the Plymouth Road in turnpike days.

The land to the east was Randall's Nurseries until 1914, when it was advertised as "ripe for immediate development, being in the centre of a populous neighbourhood, with the Trams running in front of the Property . . ."

After the war the new steeply-pitched church of St. Andrew's was built on the site of Gabriel's wood-yard on the main road. It was designed by Lucas, Roberts & Brown, and consecrated by Bishop Mortimer on 16th February 1963 (8 on map).

On the other side of Alphington Road, Nos. 6 and 8 are early 19th century houses and even Nos. 36 to 46 are semi-detached from about 1830. Each has a plain classical doorway at the side, niches and pilasters, and a hipped slate roof.

The Crawford Hotel marks the limit of the 1960 floods. It was a country farm house until 1938, when the City Brewery converted it into "the best equipped hotel of its size in the City," opened on 25th October 1939. Crawford was the farmer's name but the 1960s sign shows the arms of the Earl of Crawford.

Marsh Barton industrial estate began in 1948 when the council forcibly acquired 48 acres from the farmer Mr Newbery. The cattle market was moved from Bonhay Road in 1959, the new premises being regarded as superlative at the time. Thirty years

The Crawford Hotel

Hatherleigh House and Devon Cottage

later they seem inadequate and a new cattle market is being built at Matford. Meanwhile the industrial estate has grown vastly in 40 years and has its own link-road to the A379.

The Seven Stars, an inn which had played a great role for centuries next to Exe Bridge, was rebuilt here in 1960 to serve farmers using the cattle-market. The sign shows a cow with seven stars on its horns.

Hatherleigh House and Devon Cottage are listed buildings with thatched roofs and interesting porches. They are believed to be 400 years old in part.

St Thomas High School was built on orchard land in 1964 as part of Exeter's pioneering policy of educating 12-16 year olds separately in large comprehensives. In 1988 an arts centre with a theatre was built, to be shared with the local community.

There are several 15th-century granite boundary-crosses in our area. Alphington Cross is the finest, with its original base, octagonal shaft and arms, and a small cross incised in the centre. It stood at the crossroads until a cart crashed into it in 1830. The rector of Alphington had it repaired and re-erected at the roadside. It was moved to its present garden when the roundabout was built (9 on map).

The rise in ground-level which sets Cowick Lane above the old marshes is clearly demonstrated by the "step" in the grass on the roundabout. A handsome group of villas was built on the low ridge in the late 18th century. The Cross House is set at right angles to the road. It has three-light Gothic windows upstairs and 19th-century bays on the ground floor. Rock House has a wide 18th-century doorway. The villa has a Greek Doric porch facing the garden; the north doorway has a hood

Alphington Manor House

with elaborately carved brackets. The Exe College of English occupies the Manor House (previously Alphington House). It has two Adam fireplaces, a rococo ceiling, original fitted bedroom cupboards, and garden walls of stone and cob, and some curved screen walls with vases. It was altered about 1840, the front stuccoed and the porch moved to the side. The house is said to have been the residence of the man who broke the bank at Monte Carlo in 1891, Charles Deville Wells. A George Wells did live here in 1892-94.

Saint Hill was originally part of the Manor House. It has a Corinthian porch, a late 18th-century summerhouse and quatrefoil windows.

These houses originally enjoyed a peaceful southern outlook over the Alphin valley. The brook now shares its meadows with the constant swish of traffic on the A30, but Balls Farm Road is still a rural lane, with wild roses and cow-parsley, riding-stables and strawberry fields. It leads to two interesting houses: *The Briars* has a stucco front which is "an extreme example of mid-19th-century Gothic." *Underwood* is a thatched "cottage orné" modernised in 1972.

We turn off before the latter, up the road by the strawberry-field on the hillside and climb to the ridge-top path. The line of an old footpath leads from here to Pinces Gardens, sometimes in the form of a road, sometimes an alley way. The little footpath to Newhayes Close was the line of Cowick Lane until it was straightened out in 1920. It carried the border of the County and Parliamentary borough. We come out into Wellington Road, passing the Cowick Barton Playing Fields.

Pince's Gardens (10 on map) and the Pince's Field allotments have inherited rich soil and mature trees from the Exeter Nursery (founded in 1720 by William Lucombe), birthplace of the Exeter or Lucombe Oak. Thomas Lucombe found that an acorn from a Turkey Oak pollinated by an adjacent Cork Oak grew so straight and rapidly, with such handsome, glossy, over-wintering leaves, that he could sell thousands of cuttings in the first seven years of availability, 1765-72. They grew as tall in 20-30 years as a common oak in a century. An Exeter Oak at Cowley Place in 1957 was the tallest oak recorded in Britain, at 126 feet. William had the first oak felled to provide planks for his coffin, and kept them seasoning under his bed; but as the years went by they were used for something else, and a younger Lucombe Oak was used when he died a centenarian.

The firm later added the name of Pince from a grandson, and by 1884 the nursery was one of the sights of Exeter, taking up more than six pages in Besley's Guide: "All respectable persons are freely admitted by merely leaving their cards and addresses in the office at the entrance... There is a little town of glass... Palms, Camellias 20 ft. high, Orchids, Grape Vines... A Rock Garden where nearly every jutting crag or rounded boulder affords root-hold or shelter to some distinctive kind of vegetation. The walks wind mysteriously under sombre yews and other evergreens, and here and there open spaces, trickling rills and limpid pools afford room for the more hardy exotic plants... Bambus, Pampas Grass, Yuccas ... A quarter-mile Coniferous walk intersects the nursery, with views of the city, cathedral and spires. In the centre of the Italian garden is a wire-covered walk, over which climbing Roses, Clematises, Wistarias and other suitable plants are trained."

The nursery-ground is now a public park but still boasts the elegant pergola covered with wistaria, and the Coniferous Walk. The land was auctioned in 1912, but only a small corner was built on, just after the 1914-18 war, the delightful "Pince's Gardens" with cottagey terraces round a village-green.

A postman's nightmare, Pince's Road is right next to Princes Street. Earlier this century, Princes Square held the glasshouses of Coombes' nursery.

The travel agency in Sydney Road occupies the premises of the former dairy and off-licence called the Freehold Dairy. The streets here had been "laid out in an uniform plan in detached villas and dwellings by the Freehold Land Society" in 1876. No house was to be erected of less value than £10 per annum, or ever afterwards "used as a Shop Music or Dancing Hall Auction or other room for Public Assembly or as an Hotel Tavern Public House Beer or Coffee House or any erection thereon used for Livery or Public Stables or for any manufacture trade or commerce or any other than a Private dwelling house." They are lucky to have a post-office.

St Thomas First School (11 on map) was built in 1872. It was the first school built in the St Thomas district from public monies. R. M. Fulford designed the soaring polychrome Gothic walls with plate tracery windows. It was opened on 21st July 1873 by Bishop Temple. In 1987 the building was modernised, and the children's safety was safeguarded by blocking off two adjacent roads. Queen's Road has also been shut to traffic at its eastern end.

Homeclyst House was opened in 1987 on the site of Sydney House. The adjacent Sydney Place has individual lattice balconies at the first-floor windows, and Coade keystones over the doors. The next terrace, Hampden Place, also dates from the early 19th century, but is stuccoed, with honeysuckle capitals and a Greek-key fret above the first-floor pilasters. The city council demolished Nos. 1 and 2 to improve the exit from Haven Road, which the county council later re-aligned anyway. The terrace was sold in 1980 and converted into ten maisonettes. Behind it, the last Floyer mansion of 1770 gave way to new "Georgian" houses. Floyer descendants had lived in its 22 rooms in draughty splendour in the 1920s. Only the garden wall with granite balls still stands (12 on map).

The 18th-century stone building across the stump of old Haven Road is Pym's warehouse, a former workshop (13 on map).

We start at St Thomas railway station (1 on map). Its upper buildings and glass roof were dismantled in the 1970s. Only the ground-level offices of Brunel's South Devon Railway were preserved. They now house Fergie's Restaurant. The limestone-and-brick viaduct carried a single line from 1846 until widened in 1861. The arches face their own replicas incorporated into the design of Sainsbury's, opened in March 1986 with 25 computerised check-outs and 350 parking spaces. Lawns, domed glass arcades and spherical lamps help loosen the purse-strings. The adjacent new public library has cream walls split by an angular protruding window running up the full height of the side and across the roof like a Mohican hair-cut.

Beyond the railway-bridge is the shopping precinct built in 1972, the first local shopping scheme designed for car-owners. Parking for 100 cars was provided by demolishing picturesque old houses, shops and court-yarded Elizabethan inns, including the *Turk's Head* and the *Moreton Inn.*

For centuries they faced a thick-walled stone house built by John Holland, Duke of Exeter in the 14th century, named Beaufort after his wife's family (2 on map). From 1634 it was used as a prison. No trace of it remains except the name of Beaufort Road behind the modern shops.

The Sheriff's Ward, the county prison for debtors, was rebuilt on the north side of the street in 1818, "strong and capacious, in every way calculated for health and convenience." Only the entrance block has been kept (3 on map), brick with vermiculated quoins, segmental granite arch and brick arch above. In January 1855 the debtors were moved to the County Gaol, and the building became militia barracks. Soldiers in pill-box hats paraded in the yard at the rear. In this century

St Thomas Public Library

St Thomas Railway Station 1904, showing Brunel's roof

the building was divided into rented flats. It was demolished in the early 1970s.

The wide pavement between Buller Road and the Pleasure Ground was shaded by plane trees until after the Second World War. They were felled to save sweeping up the leaves. Nos. 35-43 are houses built about 1810 (cherub's head keystone on No. 39). Nos. 44-45 are 18th-century cottages with plastered fronts and small sash windows; the rear wing is cob and timber-frame. No. 46, the tobacconist, was previously the *Pack Horse Inn. The Prince Albert* used to be the *Lamb and Flag.*

In the year of Queen Victoria's Jubilee, it was decided to provide a safe playground for local children. Four years later, on 30th March 1891, the St Thomas People's Park was opened, with music from the Post Office Band, and a speech from the chairman of the local Board of Health about not damaging the shrubs. One acre was reserved for adults to use on Saturdays. Children could play on the other three acres.

St Thomas had its own fire brigade from July 1889. An Engine House was provided in the red-brick Council Offices built in 1898. Within two years the offices were redundant as St Thomas became part of Exeter. They were used by the County Library and then Bartlett's Printing Works until the Senior Citizens' Club took over the premises. This club had begun in 1960 in a hut in the station yard, and moved to Merrivale Road, before coming here. Founder-members Evelyn Holding and the Revd Robert Mould were still active 28 years later when Age Concern took over.

The parish church (4 on map) is built of red local stone. The nave, south aisle and slim pinnacled tower date from the 1657 re-building, so this is not the tower that the rebel vicar dangled

Gateway of Sheriff's Ward

Council Offices and Fire Station

on. In the 1820s the vicar John Coplestone and lay rector Buller decided to enlarge the church. The north aisle and porch were added in 1821. In 1828-30 the chancel was re-built, and lofty transepts with extra gallery seats were added. The odd roof-line shows where the new taller parts awkwardly abut the old. The churchyard was also extended by half an acre in 1830.

From 1838 to 1845 the vicar was John Medley, promoter of Pugin's Gothic revival. He re-designed the sanctuary and begged the eagle lectern from the Cathedral, where it had been put aside as old-fashioned. Rightly: its elaborate base from about 1320 is the oldest surviving cathedral lectern. In 1841 Medley's wife Christiana died aged 34. Her father was the sculptor John Bacon Jr. (1777-1859). He came out of retirement to carve a loving likeness of her sleeping form, and a memorial in medieval style was placed north of the altar.

The large churchyard is shaded by tall deciduous trees as well as funereal cedars and yews. Church almshouses formerly bordered the road. Most of the gravestones have been cleared to provide lawns. The Snow family tomb still stands near the south wall, near the stone listing John Stocker's services to his community.

In 1848 a man from Leeds called Thomas Gray aged 61 was buried in the churchyard. In 1818 he had tried to interest the government in a railway network, to transport soldiers, goods, passengers and letters "without the necessity of horses." The inscription on his vault read "The original projector of Grand Trunk Railways throughout Great Britain and Ireland with Direct and Level Lines." He died in poverty in a house in Alphington Road, within sight of Brunel's railway.

From the Station at St Thomas to the Alphington Meadows. View South of the Line.

St Thomas's Street and the South Devon Railway Station from the Viaduct.

The church hall is called the Buller Hall. The Bullers were the principal landowners from 1739, lords of the manor in Cowick, Exwick and Barley. They had married into the Courtenay family in the 16th century, and a child born in 1839 was named Redvers after a Norman soldier ancestor. He duly became Major General the Rt Hon Sir Redvers Buller, commanding the British forces in South Africa at the outbreak of the Boer War. He died in 1908. The hall was built in 1915 in his memory. The façade bears two coats of arms, Becket's and Buller's.

The vicarage was built for Mr Coplestone in 1800-05. It has a large two-storey bow facing the garden, which is enclosed with slate-roofed cob walls.

Old Vicarage Road was the point regularly reached by the floods. Part of the 1657 vicarage stood on the corner site until it was cleared in 1935 for the petrol station.

No. 67 (5 on map) is probably an old farmhouse. Ancient chaff still lies under the floorboards. The lower walls are cob, with lath and plaster upstairs. John Stocker's house, Nos. 65-66, has been demolished, along with the many small courts that led off Cowick Street. The modern blocks of Prospect Place preserve the name of one such court. Hill's Court ran alongside No. 67. There were cottages on the left, toilets opposite, fruit trees behind. The ring is still in the ground where a blacksmith used to shape iron rims for wheels.

The *Sawyers Arms* was a small cottage selling beer when the brewers took it over in 1911. It was re-built in 1966 on this new site. The interior is decorated with sawtooth and circular-saw motifs, and glazed tiles depicting sawing and other crafts.

The Health Centre was opened by Mayor Hallett on 7th October 1969. It was the first such centre in Exeter, with eight to ten G.P.s sharing the premises. The car park area previously held the cottages of Victoria Court.

The Methodist Church was built in 1934 in red brick with stone dressings. The front of the site had held a large, handsome house, ramshackle by the time of the First World War. It was used to house Belgian refugees, and then was pulled down. The church was built jointly by the local Wesleyans and United Methodists. Stones were laid on 31st October by their respective representatives, Colonel Ransom Pickard and Mr. A. Jane, and also one by the Mayor. Next day was a brick-laying day for children, to start off the large hall at the rear.

Mosaic playground wall by Elaine Goodwin

Cowick Street School (6 on map) had a foundation-stone laid on 31st October 1861. It opened in 1862 as St Thomas National School, with three staff to teach about 300 boys and girls, with the aid of untrained pupil-teachers. It started up again in 1872 as Cowick Street Boys, then St Thomas Boys. In 1911 it was remodelled for infants and girls only. It is now a mixed First School. The playground harbours a brilliant treasure, a mosaic wall by Elaine Goodwin showing playtime through the seasons. *Take Hart* filmed it for TV, each child leaping forward from its portrayal. The children were so keen to contribute to the project that a loose tooth dislodged by school dinner was rushed outside and incorporated into the design.

Against the north wall of the school is an ancient granite cross 44 inches tall, 15 inches wide, cut from a single stone, the arms hollowed to form a double tau "cross potent." It was put here when Victoria Court was demolished for Barton Road to go through. For centuries it had marked the turning-off point for the ancient main route to Kenn and Haldon.

The *Falmouth Inn* was re-built in 1913. It has recently been re-named the *First and Last,* appropriately, as it stands at the edge of the old town. The tram terminated here, and the turnpike gate was opposite. All the turnpikes round Exeter were removed in 1884.

A horse-trough at the foot of the hill was given by Mrs. Plummer in 1924. Her husband owned Colson's (now Dingles). They lived at Crossmead and seem to have spent their journeys up and down the hill searching for opportunities for benevolence. They were married in the parish church, and paid for its bells to be restored in 1923. The vicar hoped that "for many, many years to come, the music of the bells, wafted on the breeze to Crossmead, may put them in happy remembrance of the happiest of all days." Mr (later Sir Edgar) Plummer gave £500 and the site for St Philip's mission church, which was dedicated on 30th January 1929.

The adjacent large corner site where Bowhill House had been demolished already held a new St Thomas Boys' School, opened in January 1902. The headmaster lived in the house at the corner. In 1921 the school was re-named in honour of John Stocker, alderman and J.P., who had completed 50 years on the education committee. In 1936 he had laid the stone for the present building, which housed Junior Boys and Senior Boys from 1938. It is now used for 8 to 12 year olds (7 on map).

Within living memory the hillside from here to Crossmead was covered with orchards and nurseries. Some of the road names acknowledge this: Greenway, Parkway, Orchard Gardens, Orchard Hill. The grey-stone R.C. church with its Italianate campanile was built on Kerswill's nursery-ground in 1937-38 and dedicated to St Thomas of Canterbury. The houses on Broadway were built in 1929. Greenway and Littleway stand above the busy Dunsford Road round their own little green.

Bowhill (8 on map) is an important 15th-century manor house, so important that the Historic Building and Monument Commission is rumoured to be spending another 500 years restoring it. Its glory is the wagon-roof of the Great Hall in the east wing, but the south range along the road, and part of the kitchen-wing to the west, also survive from the original quadrangle. The walls are roughly built of red Heavitree stone and volcanic trap. The house, named *Bogehull* ("curved hill") after the estate, was started in 1422 and probably just finished when its private chapel was licensed in 1429 for Richard Holland, who was M.P. for Devon in 1430. His son and grandson also served as M.P.s for Exeter. The fine roofs of the Great Hall and of the solar in the south wing are thought to be late 15th-century, perhaps from 1488 when the Holland heiress in the next generation married a Carew. The Hall has four large square-headed windows with external decorations of carved human heads and internal signs that shutters were used. There was a screen in the south range which has lost its panelling but retains the original moulded doorways with pointed arches. The large kitchen fireplace also survives, with a joggled segmental stone arch. (How many fitted kitchens from the 1980s will last five centuries?)

The Carews held the manor for many generations, although John the regicide forfeited the honour and his life in 1661. In 1662 Charles II restored the manor to Thomas. He had no sons, and the property passed to the Sawle family by marriage. In 1792 the surrounding land was sold. In 1799 the house itself was sold to be used for the new St Thomas Hospital for Lunatics, accommodating 15 patients. This institution soon erected its own buildings lower down the hillside.

At one time, Bowhill was the residence of the grand-parents of General Gordon of Khartoum. On 18th January 1884 he was in the porch of the parish church, about to visit their memorial, when he was summoned to London and thence to his martyrdom in the Moslem uprising. For the past century or so, Bowhill has been an ordinary farmhouse, the Great Chamber partitioned, the Great Hall given an extra floor to store many tons of apples, and the chapel used as a barn. The Sclater family ran the extensive Bowhill nurseries and orchards for several generations. The fields were covered with

houses in the late 1950s, with streets named after counties. In 1958 the Baptists bought a corner site on this estate for a church, and laid the foundation stone on 28th April 1962. They built in red brick to match the houses, installed the pews from their 1884 church in Bartholomew Street, and opened on 16th February 1963 (9 on map).

Above the path to Cowick Hill on the south side of Dunsford Road is a reservoir built about 1870. Water was pumped up to it by the engine in Buller Road.

At the top of Dunsford Road there is a superb view over Exeter. An ancient ridgeway ran along the line of Hambeer Lane and Barley Lane. In the 1920s rain washed a silver coin from a Barley Lane hedgebank, a Roman coin dropped on the old trackway.

Tulip time in Bowhill orchards

A granite boundary-cross (74 inches high, 26 inches wide) stands inside the garden wall on the corner of the lane to Ide (10 on map). Only the lower half of the cross is 15th-century. It used to stand against the hedge by the main road. When the assize judges moved on from Exeter to Bodmin, their carriage was escorted to this point by the Sheriff's javelin men, led by their Captain on horseback dressed in a scarlet coat and cocked hat. The name Little John's Cross has echoes of the beloved disciple or of Robin Hood's companion, but we must remember that a local family was called Littlejohn, and the cross probably stood at the corner of their land. A John Littlejohn connected with the Barley family is recorded from 1402.

The cross probably gave the name to the field at the north-west corner of the junction, where a row of three stucco villas was built in 1829 and called simply Nos. 1, 2 and 3 Crossmead. They stand at right angles to the road to catch the view. Less massive than Pennsylvania Park, they are comparable in site and style. They have verandahed balconies with slender iron supports standing firmly on semi-basements in two of the houses. All three have slate roofs with wide eaves, side doorways, one with Greek-key-patterning, and sash windows. A one-storey lodge with splayed end stands opposite.

The name Crossmead is now used for the large Victorian mansion built about 1893 by Mr James Langdon Thomas. It was acquired by the University College of the South West in 1944, but the Fire Service occupied it until the end of the war. It became a student hall of residence, later adding a modern bedroom block. It is now a well-equipped conference centre, surrounded by mature trees, blue spruces round the lily pond and scarlet chestnuts lining the drive.

The Royal Masonic Benevolent Institution have built a large retirement home on the corner. The communal rooms form a central doughnut shape. Three substantial wings complete a "propeller" lay-out. The development was opened and named on 1st October 1987 by the Earl Cadogan.

Exonia Park nestles in the sun-trap of the disused quarries. Blasting stopped in the 1930s, and the land was used for a market garden for a time. The cliff-face shows the characteristic white-veined reddish-mauve of the Pocombe stone, which is a volcanic basalt like Rougemont. Semi-permanent "mobile" homes with pretty gardens now stand on winding lanes called after birds: Sandpiper Green, Swallow Drive etc. Eagles' Nest is a grass-verged promenade along the western fringe with beautiful views over green hills. On 1st April 1988 the boundary of Teignbridge moved South West to the motor-way, and this area was welcomed into Exeter.

Crossmead Villas

Walking along Polsloe Road these days gives one very little feeling of being on a prehistoric ridgeway route, nor does Sidwell Street bear much resemblance to the muddy track it was in the Middle Ages. However, climbing Hambeer Lane, walking between hedges just below the crest of the ridge, does convey a little of the nature of ancient pathways. A network of them straddles the ridge, from the days when everyone went on two feet or four, and were well aware of the gradients. It was worth avoiding the steep slope by Crossmead. There is an intriguing kink as Hambeer Lane passes a prominent hillock. Was that a prehistoric assembly-point? A look-out? A beacon?

We turn left where the footpath from Ide crosses our path. In 1930 Colonel Ransom Pickard suggested that this footpath was the main track from Exeter to all the country west of Exeter, leading to the crossing of the Teign. Take care that you come back to the 20th century before you cross busy Cowick Lane.

Cowick Barton public house (11 on map) is the mansion built for Russell about 1540 after he dissolved St Andrew's Priory, doubtless re-using the stones. It has mullioned windows and a Tudor-arched entrance to the projecting three-storey porch in the centre. Short wings at each end are probably later additions. Lord Russell had a town house in the city, so Cowick was probably built for his bailiff. It remained in the Bedford family for a hundred years, passing to the Pate family in 1641. An ornate overmantel dated 1657 commemorated some now-forgotten event. A more intriguing plaster relief forms the overmantel in the function room in the east wing. On the left a nun or the Blessed Virgin is caring for several children, on the right is a maiden with long hair, each standing on the head of a fat doll-like friar. Three children in

medieval costume are being led by an angel and dragged back by a little devil. There is a cryptic Bible reference — "Phil. III, 14" which has been interpreted as a coded instruction to activate a secret panel to a priest-hole: "I press towards the mark." Under the carpet there is a trap-door leading to cellars and passages. Robert Pate and his son each left annuities payable out of the Barton of Cowick for a school-mistress to teach four poor children. Perhaps this was a school-room.

The Pate family passed the property down to a Mr James White by 1830, and it remained for five generations with Whites, or White Abbots. John White Abbott (1763-1851) was a surgeon and a fine water-colourist, who painted Devon views, some held in the Exeter Museum. He will have appreciated the rural surroundings of the Barton. The Revd John Swete described them in September 1789: "On the northern side of this House is a grove of uncommonly large Elms. Through a break amid the successive ranges of Elms, Exeter is beheld, with its turreted Cathedral, rising with lordly grandeur over the subjacent city."

13th-century remains of the Priory were found east of the house when drains were dug in 1887. White Abbott's grandson and namesake carefully restored the house in 1895.

The "Agricultural Property" of Cowick Barton was sold by auction in 1920. It comprised 75 acres divided by Cowick Lane, and the Barton House with its extensive range of farm outbuildings, some of which still stand to one side of the car park: "Five-stall Stable and Loose Box, Four-stall Cow House and Root House, 12-stall Cow House, Hay House, Piggery and Slaughter House, Barns, Bullock House with loft over, and Double Cow Shed for Ten. Brick Cart Shed with corrugated-iron Roof. Granary on stone piers, wood with slate roofing."

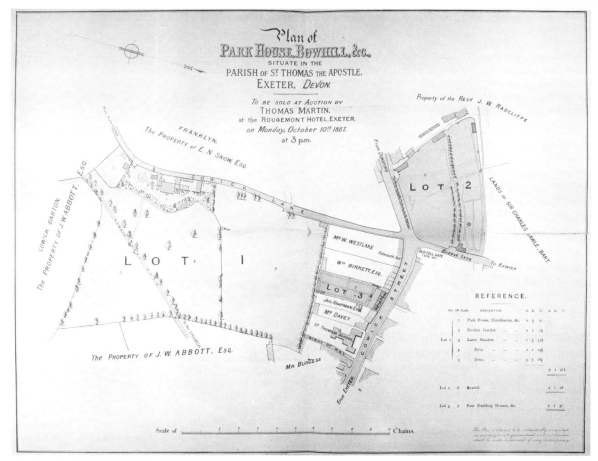

D.R.O. 62/9/2/BOX 11/58

The brewery acquired the house in 1963 and opened up the car-park and garden.

In 1789 John Swete had also "past before Franklin, a seat of Counsellor Fanshawes, embosomed in groves of noble Elms" (12 on map). This is a handsome, square, two-storey, William and Mary house with a hipped slate roof. The ornate doorway has Corinthian pilasters, scrolled pediment and cartouche. There is one excellent ceiling, and a fine staircase, with carved vases and flowers on the newel caps (boarded in at present). The house was named from its first owner, but passed by marriage to Jasper Radcliffe and then to his son Walter (died 1751). In 1757 rainwater gutters were added. From about 1825 to 1925 a branch of the ubiquitous Snow family lived here. From 1928-57 the house was the Home of the Holy Innocents, then Franklyn House Hospital. It was altered and extended in 1972.

The roads between Cowick Lane and Barton Road occupy the former grounds of Park House, which was offered for sale in 1887 with the following eulogy: "No expense has been spared in fitting the house from time to time with every convenience of the most modern improvement. The WC is fitted with a Tyler & Sons Patent Flush Pan. There is a bountiful supply of pure Spring and 'Exeter Corporation' Water and outer Yard with Shed, Piggery and Servants WC. The sanitary arrangements are perfect. A bathroom could easily be erected." Triggs, Sanders and Sleeman began to build streets of houses here in 1905. (£250 without a bathroom, £300 with — obviously a time of transition.) It is no longer easy to trace the monks' way which came down from Hambeer Lane and ran behind the parish church to the river-crossing. Earlier this century Church Path Fields still provided a pleasant walk past cows and buttercups. "The path itself was of cobble-stones with gravel on either side and a low wooden fence with wire netting." It followed the line of the present Larch Road, then straightened out and ran across to where we now have Tin Lane (officially Churchfield Path) and Church Road. Tin Lane Community Centre (13 on map) was built after World War I as a United Men's Service Club. A foundation stone was laid on 28th October 1922 by Major General Sir Edward May, Major Brock, Edgar Plummer and W. H. Reed. It now serves all sections of the community. The façade has been embellished by a mosaic illustrating the different age-groups who have fun here. This, too, was designed by Elaine Goodwin and completed by a team of volunteers.

The County Ground (14 on map) stands on land previously used for cricket, football and wrestling. Wrestling matches had generally taken place between the hay and corn harvests, on ground laid with tan. At the end of July 1841 there was a great match for the prize of 100 sovereigns. "An area of an acre and a quarter, in a circular form, in a fine and level field, near St Thomas Church, was enclosed by boarded work, one half having raised seats covered with tarpaulins, the other half a bench running round, and a gallery with a band of music."

In 1888 W H Commins put the Wrestling Field up for sale — "Important to Capitalists, Builders, Speculators and others..." — either for houses or a "much-needed Recreation Ground." Recreation won; on 14th May 1894 the Devon County Athletic Ground Co Ltd opened the grounds with a grandstand to seat 700, an elliptical cycling track, with the ground inside laid out for football or cricket. Outside, accommodation for tennis, archery and other games was in course of erection. The ground is now also used for greyhound racing, and motor-bike speedway has become increasingly popular since 1947.

A Karate club meets in a former church in Church Road, opened on 15th August 1872 as a United Methodist Free Church, architect G. Packham, and later used as a Salvation Army Hall.

On the other side of Church Road, Nos. 1-14 form a red-brick Georgian terrace, facing south, built circa 1805-10. There are still original Coade mask keystones and cast-iron balconies on the first floor. The entrances to Nos. 9 and 10 are under an arch leading to Cowick Street. Car-taming measures have been introduced in the neighbouring streets. Prince Charles would approve of this quiet residential area in easy reach of work, transport, shops and recreation.

Congregational Church, Cecil Road, built in 1901

Community Centre mosaic by Elaine Goodwin

The Seven Stars stood on the river bank close to the old bridge. It was one of sixteen Devon inns of this name near rivers, displaying the emblem of St John Nepomuk, martyred in the River Vltava by Bad King Wenceslas.

Okehampton Street is now open to the river on one side, as it was in the 1860s when (John Stocker recalled) it was lined with "the pride of the parish, a beautiful row of enormous oak trees." *The Royal Oak* continues the pun. The raised river bank protects it from floods, such as the one in 1960 that washed a cask out to sea. They know how far it went because a minesweeper brought it back two months later.

The disco hall began as assembly rooms called The King's Halls. It became a cinema, then a night-club, and now changes name nearly as often as fashions change: Riverside, Zhivago's, Routes, Power House . . .

High walls near the river bank shelter Sclaters' Victoria Nurseries, last remnant of the family's extensive chain of nurseries which for centuries surrounded the city with flowering fields and orchards.

Flowerpot (2 on map) is possibly corrupted from Floyer, its name in the Middle Ages. This corner was the site of the battle in 1643, and the less grim battle in 1986 about building on recreation land. John Lees has designed accommodation appropriate to the site, like a smart yachting-club. As the breezes blow along the towpath, it is hard to believe that the protest was based on the argument that there would be no fresh air left.

The street passes under the railway and becomes Okehampton Road. Behind Emmanuel Church (3 on map) is Emmanuel Close, with sixteen flats built by the Exeter Workmen's Dwell-

The Seven Stars and Okehampton Street, drawn by P. V. Pitman

Emmanuel Church

ing Co Ltd in 1927-31, opened by Viscountess Sidmouth. In 1887 a new parish was carved out of St Thomas to serve the new streets off Okehampton Road. Redvers Buller donated the site, and a little iron church was erected and called Emmanuel. 113 designs were submitted for a stone church; the winner was a Gothic design by Harold Brakspear. The cost was raised within ten years, thanks to "a notable contribution" from the vicar's father, Sir George Williams, founder of the YMCA. Redvers Buller laid the foundation stone in mid-October 1897 under "an awning which just sheltered it from the rays of the setting sun... The bells of the mother church rang out merry peals." After an open-air service with choir and orchestra, the ladies served tea to over 350 people at the adjacent Board Schools, with more music.

The church was built of grey limestone with a tiled roof. The interior is lined with red Pocombe stone. The planned south-west tower was too expensive, but there is a distinctive polygonal vestry at the south-east corner. Bishop Bickersteth consecrated the church on 2nd October 1900. From 1924 to 1963 Emmanuel's vicar was the Revd Ernest Francis Tozer. The church was slightly damaged in the 1942 blitz. In 1988 David Gubbin installed windows depicting St Francis, and the conversion of St Paul, in memory of Mr and Mrs Tozer.

The Vicarage, a large house on the other side of the road, had been the residence of old Mr Walton of Walton's drapery store; he would set out to business every morning in a carriage and pair. The vicarage faces the turning to the Church Hall. When the vicar's wife laid the foundation stone in October 1921, it was felt necessary to state that it would be for the parish and Sunday School, and would not be let out in competition with the larger King's Halls. Emmanuel Hall faced demolition in the 1970s, but found a new role as a branch of the Northcott Theatre, for rehearsals and small productions.

John Levers Way

Manor Road leads to Montgomery School. Alderman John Stocker laid its foundation stone on 28th October 1929, and the school was opened in 1930 by the Bishop of Plymouth. The field it stands on was previously known as the Easter Fair Field (4 on map). It was owned by Mr. Kerswell. He kept one or two Jersey cows on it for 51 weeks of the year, then on the Monday before Easter the fair would arrive, with helter-skelter, distorting mirrors, swing-boats etc. ... In 1877 a novelty was the switchback railway, which did "a roaring biz." Once Emmanuel Church was built, the congregation found the fairground organs very noisy during the Good Friday services.

John Levers Way (5 on map) is named for the popular and hard-working councillor who died prematurely in 1979. The red-brick terrace (with a startling roof-line sweeping up like wings at the corner entrance) curls round a communal back garden with a statue of a little ballerina.

The old turnpike gate stood opposite Felixwell. Felixwell is an early 19th-century white stuccoed house with a verandah, facing south-east. It contrasts with the red Pocombe stone of adjacent Redhills Hospital (6 on map), built in 1836-7 by the St Thomas Union as a County Workhouse for the old and unfortunate young of fifty parishes. The imposing three-storey building stands on rising ground. Its lay-out is like the spokes and rim of a wheel. A visitor in 1868 was impressed by the orderly and cheerful regime. Thirty-five boys had an airy attic dormitory above a schoolroom, into which the school-master could erupt through a trap-door from his sitting-room. Men were taught tailoring and shoe-making, women sewing. Girls were trained to enter service at sixteen. Old married couples were offered double bedrooms, but usually preferred wards with their own sex. The visitors noted approvingly that "the knives and forks are cleaned every day." A

Redhills Hospital

Okehampton Turnpike Gate, drawn by James Townsend

Buddle Lane resident remembers nurses wheeling prams full of babies, and walking toddlers along the lane. "On many occasions my mother poured hot water into some old tramp's drinking-tin, as he drank hot tea in the hedge, waiting for the time when he could get a bed for the night in the workhouse." Casuals used a separate entrance and had to pick a pound of oakum before leaving. Redhills now shelters only the older generation, and is under threat of closure.

The road ahead now called Redhills, was previously still "the Okehampton Road," then "the old Okehampton Road" when Dunsford Road became the main route north. In its heyday this was the road between Baldwin's two castles. Later, it was the route for the mail-coach to Falmouth. "From its steepness the turnpike trustees allowed extra horses to assist in pulling vehicles up the hill without additional toll, a painted fixed board directing where to 'put on' and 'take off'." Our walk need not include this daunting climb, but here are some features of the hill:— The earliest record of the name Red for this area is "la Rededowne" in 1264. In 1710 a will mentioned "fields called Redhill in the parish of St Thomas." Redhills Combined School was built in 1967. In 1581 there was "a close called Wylpark in Exweek." Wellpark Cottage stood here in 1890, and now there is a road called Well Park Close above the school. Benjamin Donn's map of 1765 shows a house called Red Hill on the north side of the road. Jenkins in 1806 wrote "On Red Hill is a neat, new-erected villa, commanding a delightful prospect of the City, river and adjacent country; built by John Dennis, Esq., alderman, of Exeter."

Addison Close may be named from the essayist, who was a cousin of the St Thomas classical scholar Eustace Budgell.

Hadrian Drive and Antonine Close are named after Roman emperors who built walls at the interface with the barbarians. Children who move into new houses on these slopes should read a story set here — *A Beacon for the Romans*, by David Rees. Luggs Farm nestles below the junction with Barley Lane, besieged by the rising tide of housing.

The Barley Mow was built in 1963. The bricks were selected to blend with neighbouring houses. The Barley estate was built on the slopes belonging to Barley House (7 on map). Savile Road is called after Col. J. W. Savile who lived there at the turn of this century, when there were two huge chestnut trees by the gate-keeper's lodge in Buddle Lane, and a long winding drive through the tall meadow grass of the park-lands.

If we struggle up the punishing incline of Isleworth Road, we shall understand why General Fairfax chose to garrison the Barley House of his time during his siege of Exeter in 1646. Few positions were so impregnable, with such a commanding view of the city. Charles II granted the estate to Thomas Carew, with Bowhill. A Carew heiress married John Pinnock, who rebuilt Barley House early in the 18th century. It was inherited by his nephew Richard Sawle. Richard's daughters sold Bowhill and Higher Barley in 1792, but kept the rights of carriage access to Barley. Bowhay Lane is a modern road at the Dunsford Road end, and a grassy bridleway at the Barley Lane end, and the middle section, so indispensable for the carriage-horses tackling the steep contours, survives as back alleys between High Meadows and Charnley Avenue. Elizabeth Sawle married John Graves (one of four brothers who all became admirals). She occupied Barley at the beginning of the 19th century when the Doric portico and curving stairs were added. A century later, a distant cousin lived there, blind old Walter King. He attended church in a smart carriage pulled by chestnut horses, his dalmatians running underneath. The family sold the house in the 1930s. Devon County Council purchased it in 1938 and it is now the administrative centre of Devon Library Services. A two-storey brick and glass extension was built at the south side in the mid-1960s. White doves flutter by the green-washed walls of the main house.

Buddle Lane runs along a rise in the ground where several springs of water periodically break out. In the late 1940s one burst right through the tarmacadam. Buddle Lane was sometimes called Pound Lane after the pound for stray animals at the southern end. Nos. 94-128 form a Victorian terrace, occupied when new mostly by railway families.

Once, in about 1920, Devon County Show was held in Mr. Littlejohn's field. Bulls, cows, sheep and horses came from St David's station, and a great crowd of farmers, carts, stock and traps. The lane remained rural until about 1923, when the council built 64 houses for people moving from back-to-back slums in the city. The present occupants have the benefit of the Buddle Lane Family Unit nursery centre in Merrivale Road, where the King of Spain's daughter helped teach in 1988 as part of her child-psychology course at Exeter University.

There is a record of "Broadparks in Exweek" in 1590, and "six closes called broadparks" in 1735. "Broadmeadow Cottages" stood on Buddle Lane in the 1890s. The City Brewery bought a site on the Broadmeadow building estate and opened *Green Gables* in June 1935.

We turn downhill before this, down a path to Maple Road, Clarence Road and into Buller Road. The red-brick building used as offices for Watts' Garage was a pumping-station for the St Thomas waterworks (8 on map). Well-water (supplemented by river-water piped from the banks opposite St David's Station) was pumped from here to the filter beds by Dunsford Road. After 1902 St Thomas was supplied from Pynes. The tall tower of this pumping-station stood for a further 27 years before being demolished.

We turn towards Cowick Street. Wippell's is an old Exeter family firm, established about 200 years ago, specializing for the last 150 years in clerical outfitting and church furnishings. The factory was built for Heathcote's Lace Company but never used by them. The alley opposite, behind the Shopping Centre, is on the line of the old Rope Walk (9 on map) where ropes were twisted by hand. Bell-ropes had coloured wool twisted in. Apple-trees grew here in living memory. In 1853 there was a potato-patch by the viaduct, into which a traveller fell unharmed when he stepped out of the train too soon.

Pumping Station

We start at the level-crossing (1 on map). When Mallett ran Exwick Mills, he had to pay a toll to the railway every time he fetched grain from the station. He listed the tolls paid in one week in June to see if it was worth building his own bridge:—

		s.	d.
13	2-horse Waggons @ 9d	9.	9
1	3-horse Waggon	1.	1½
28	1-horse or cabs @ 7d	16.	4
41	2-wheel Traps or Carts @ 4½d	15.	4½
18	horses @ 1d	1.	6
14	Perambulators and 3-wheel Barrows @ 2d	2.	4
12	single-wheel Barrows @ 1d	1.	0
20	Bicycles @ 2d	3.	4
6	Bullocks 1d head		6
	Week Total	£2. 11.	3

Cyclists today are luckier; no tuppenny toll to use the Cycle Path, a safe flat route to Exe Bridges and beyond, inaugurated on 17th June 1988 by Peter Bottomley. It is one of six schemes subsidised by the Government.

A much larger undertaking was the Flood Prevention Scheme. After the 1960 floods, experts recommended digging two tunnels 3½ miles long and as high as a house, through the rock that Exeter stands on; or else re-design the river. Put like that, Plan B sounded sensible, though the vast expense — £4 million — made some wonder whether it might be cheaper to re-house the entire population on higher ground.

In 1973 Devon River Authority started digging a mile-long relief channel, straightening the river, and filling in Exwick Leat between Higher Mill and the river. This work may have helped cause the devastating damage in September 1974. Harold Ackland remembers gazing fascinated as the flood waters demolished Station Road. "The water was that rapid and that forceful you could see it washing a whole circle out of the field. The force of the water literally ate that field out. You could see lumps just dropping into the water — hunks as high as this table — and then it washed out the next part. No machine could clear earth like that. I told the inspector he would be back by 12 o'clock ordering a new bridge over the river. The bridge collapsed at 11.30 p.m." Last across were G.P.O. engineers, to cut the telephone lines. Next day the connection was restored by coastguards firing a lifeline. St Andrew's Flower Festival did an unusually brisk trade. Two years later the Army lowered into place the present single-span road-bridge. It is designed to tilt to meet any bridge which ever replaces the level-crossing.

The Flood Relief Channel is used by anglers and model-boaters. The banks of stone-filled gabions are covered with turf which can be replaced if a flood scours it away. Twin sluice-gates bridge the river (2 on map). If the level rises, they close automatically, sending the flow sideways over a weir. The scheme was opened on 23rd September 1977 by John Silkin.

The old "Path Meadow" is Exwick's recreation ground, scene in June 1988 of Swan Fair, culmination of a week of community pageants. Giant representations of the River Exe and a feathery swan moved among children dancing with paper fishes on their heads, blue streamers rippling behind. "General Buller" pranced on a green hobby-horse. The Exwick Institution, or Parish Hall, was built in memory of the 1914-18 war, from £1 subscriptions. Redvers Buller gave the site. The Bullers had also given land for the village school, in 1859.

St Andrew's Church, Exwick

When the new school was built in 1971, the old building became a community centre. The Parish Hall, Community Centre and Parish Church play a vital role as the new estates bring a population explosion, with a high proportion of under-fives and a rapid turnover of young families in starter-homes.

On the corner is the old toll-house for the turnpike road. The hook that held a chain across Exwick Road is still there. However, the villagers could go to church without passing it, and the priest coming across the fields from St Thomas also avoided the toll by using a side entrance.

St Andrew's (3 on map) looks unexceptional to us, accustomed as we are to Victorian Gothic, but in 1842 it was hailed by the Camden Society as "the best example of a modern church we have yet seen." It was built as a small chapel-of-ease with chancel, nave, south porch and bell-gablet; a north-west spire was designed but never built. The stone altar, reredos and font were small versions of those in St Thomas, reflecting the enthusiasm of the Revd John Medley. Thirty years later another determined man left his mark on the building. William Gibbs of Tyntesfield had already borne the expense of St Michael's Church and Cowley Chapel and a chapel for Keble College. Now he begged Buller to sell him the Exwick living, and make it independent of St Thomas. In 1873 he brought back the original architect, Hayward, to lengthen the chancel and add a north aisle, behind polished marble pillars crowned with lilies and passion-flowers. Panels illustrating the Benedicite were stencilled on the chancel ceiling, and a dado of musicians along the wall. William Gibbs also paid for a substantial stone house for the new vicar, William Cobham Gibbs. This stands high above Exwick Road, and has been the Diocesan Training Centre since 1983, re-named Mercer House after Bishop Eric. It made a huge vicarage, with private chapel, dairy with cool slate shelves, and stables on Exwick Hill.

The Village Inn was known as *The Lamb* from 1850-1987, and before that *The John Bull*. The original inn, recorded in the 15th century, was part of the old Exwick manor-house, of which only the stone garden wall remains. The manor had passed from the monks to the Russells and then the Olivers. In the 1780s the house was sold to Banfill and Granger, together with several acres of farmland. They transformed the hamlet into an industrial area. There had been medieval grist and fulling mills on the leat. A paper-mill mentioned in 1673 was one of the earliest in England. But the new factory buildings spread from the leat to the lane and up the north side of Exwick Hill. A Dye House and Washing House were built east of the lane. A new Exwick House (4 on map) was also

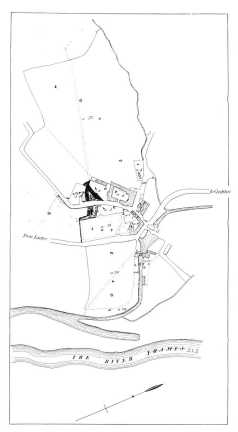

1830 auction brochure prepared in London.
D.R.O. 2065m/T2/9

built here in about 1820 with Ionic porch and tall ground-floor sash-windows facing the river-meadows. When Banfill retired to the Hermitage in 1830, it was advertised as having "every requisite for a family of the first respectability." Lower Mills were eventually taken over by the County Laundry, but when they burnt down in 1942-3, it used Exwick House until 1980. In 1982 the laundry outbuildings were cleared, the old water-wheel was cut up, Exwick House was divided into flats, and terraces of small houses were built in its grounds.

We follow St Andrew's Road to the Higher Mills, passing Exwick Farm (bereft of its fields) and various features called after the next farm, Hamlyns. Hamlyns Lane, hidden between hedges next to a private garage, is an ancient footpath and pack-horse route to Whitestone Church. It twists and turns, in places through solid rock. In 1939, Tom Greenslade of The Knap suggested that it would make an ideal trench shelter for the ARP. Hamlyns House was built by mill-owner Mallett in 1903. The balustrades each side of the entrance came from the Exe Bridge demolished in that year. Hamlyns Farm has a massive barn bordering the road. The name goes back to 16th-century tenants.

Exwick Mill (5 on map) stands over the leat that powered the Saxon mill mentioned in Domesday, then the mills run by St Andrew's monks and later ones that stood until 1886. In that year Mallett had Banfill's Higher Woollen Mill demolished and replaced with the present five-storey red-brick edifice, and installed huge new machines, including a Semolina Purifier for all those Victorian milk-puddings. Taylor & Bodley of Exeter made an enormous steel Poncelet water-wheel, the widest in Britain. The mill supplied self-raising flour for the baking trade until 1958. For over a thousand years the mill had run mostly on water-power, supplemented occasionally with electricity.

The present owner, Dick Pennell, is carefully restoring the building, which is used for storage, for rock-bands to rehearse, and for the Tools for Self-reliance group to re-cycle hand-tools for Africa. Another part of the mill is used by a garden-centre, reached by a bridge of stone salvaged from Ide Rectory in 1979.

Our walk turns back to Exwick, but the following landmarks lie further up the road. Cott Farm, with ducks in the yard and lucky horse-shoes over the shed-doors, was once part of the endowment of the Atwill and Grendon charities. They advertised it in 1922 as "admirably situated for a Dairy or Fruit Farm, or for a small Pleasure Farm." This part of the valley remains unspoilt. Earlier this century it seemed a paradise to Mr Ackland when he moved here from Newtown, having courted, and eventually married, Rhona, a local lass. He would creep out at 5 am or 6 am when the haze was on the meadows. "The sun's rays would shine down through gaps in the coverage of leaves. Kingfishers would flash down, even sit on your rod. Six or eight herons — they all had their own area — stood in the field on the side of the leat; suddenly one would tilt forward, and stand up again with a fish in his beak." The pool under the weir at Foghay was a favoured fishing spot. The name Voggeheyes is recorded as early as the 11th century, when the weir was first built, and probably refers to the coarse grass, not the river mist. See the two entries for fog in Chambers Dictionary.

Weircliffe House was described by Jenkins in 1806 as "a neat cottage, built on the edge of a clift, hanging over the river; underneath are waving walks cut out of the rock, and beautifully overhung by trees and coppice wood, in a most romantic manner; the roaring of the river below, over an artificial ware, the hanging cliffs etc., are very pleasing; this cottage was built,

and the improvements to the natural beauties of the spot, designed by John Merivale Esq. of Barton-Place." He will have looked across to this house from Barton Place. His only son John Herman Merivale (1779-1844), a friend of Byron, wrote these lines:

> "Yet poets, too by Isca dream;
> Rich meadows kiss her sparkling face,
> And ancient walls o'erhang her stream,
> And peopled towns her borders grace."

His second son was the well-known historian of the Roman Empire. Which generation does Merivale Road celebrate?

Cowley Bridge stands at a very ancient crossing-point, where the Creedy and the Exe run close together to pass between the hills into the same valley. A bridge is recorded in 1286. After the floods of 1809 and 1810 brought down the stone bridge, James Green, the County Surveyor, designed the present handsome structure, with its three segmental arches and niched piers, and it was built in 1813-14.

We turn back to Kinnerton Way, which runs along the floor of a valley, deceptively promising easy access to the buildings which fringe the skyline like Indians waiting to attack. Pedestrians face daunting climbs up several flights of concrete steps. Having Liffey Rise lead to Guinness Lane is a stout Irish joke. This estate was built by the Guinness Trust. The steep fields of Exwick Farm were not developed without controversy. Pennsylvania and Duryard residents objected to the threat to their green view. (The new houses have a pleasant green view of Pennsylvania and Duryard.) Local people warned that the hill-top was a swamp. The developers tried pumping and eventually built on rafts. The spring at the foot of the hill ran non-stop into the restored horse-trough.

View from Guinness Lane

Mallison Close commemorates a professor who left his money to the city. He had taught maths at the University for many years, even after his sight failed, when his wife had to guide him and write on the blackboard. The council estate at the northern end of Kinnerton Way was built in 1988-89 like a hill-top village. Red brick is enlivened with semi-circular courses in yellow. Children play in the sheltered streets, which could easily be freed from motor traffic by restricting it to the main access road.

Exwick Hill is the picturesque heart of the old village. Its houses do not change hands as rapidly as the ones on the new estates. The corner was re-built with half-timbering and a turret in 1893, with a shop and Post Office at No. 1. Numbers 3, 5, 7 and 9 seem almost built into the hill, with deep recessed windows in solid stone walls.

Rackfield Cottages were owned by Mallett and named after the field where cloth was stretched on racks to dry. "Coming up Exwick Hill today one can still trace the possible position of the buildings in use in 1792. At one side of the Square are two cottages which still have cellars underneath, doubtless the vaults to the Sulphur or Bleaching House. The rest of the Square together with the site of the present Eaton House was covered by the Press Shop, the Callender Shops where the material was smoothed under rollers, the Packing Shops, the Whisking and Burling Shops, for winding yarn and dressing the cloth, the Rowing Rooms where the nap was put on, the Furnishing Rooms, the Warehouses, Cloth Houses and Cloth Room."

The Hermitage

The Hermitage (6 on map) is a charming, rambling cottage *orné*, thatched, its two wings forming a V-shape. The east wing was a 16th-century cottage, of which the front section was even older, with cruck structure and a bulging bread-oven. This part may have been the chamber which the Priory could not afford to repair in the early 15th century. Banfill retired to this cottage in 1830, and had it knocked through to the neighbouring cottage, forming the Hermitage as it is now, its architecture ranging from the low-ceilinged, heavily beamed room in the east to the late Regency drawing room at the west end, with its 19th-century leaded Gothic casements. Samuel Banfill died here in 1843 aged 81. In 1878 it was the home of the prolific playwright Henry Arthur Jones (1851-1929), friend of Pinero, G.B.S. and Beerbohm. The Theatre Royal, Exeter, was the first to stage his plays, giving him the confidence to retire from commercial travelling.

No. 22, above the Hermitage, has a brick-and-cob gabled front, 18th-century sash, gabled hood to door. The cob cottages behind, with window shutters, complete the picturesque group. Nos. 1 and 2 have early panelled doors. Exwick Hill has been shut to traffic above this section, to protect the narrow road from the countless car-drivers who have settled on the new estates.

If we walk past Exwick School and up a rural lane, we pass behind the Guide Dog kennels to the back of Cleve House (7 on map). Cleave, Cleve, Cliffe or Great Cleave is an old estate sited below a strong spring of water. John de Nethere-clyve is recorded in 1339. It passed down in the family of Joel de Buckington and came to John Holland. In the early 1600s it was occupied by Thomas Malet, then Zenobia Mallet, then owned by Benjamin Oliver, followed by Robert Gubbs. The estate was purchased by a Thomas Northmore in the reign of Charles II; his heir and namesake was MP for Okehampton; he extended the house, and died in 1713.

Some of the interior dates from Gubbs' time. Northmore's house was L-shaped, the long main wing being two rooms deep and two storeys high, each with seven windows looking across a flat meadow towards Duryard. Some of the plaster ceilings date from the late 17th century. The façade was altered in the late 18th century, adding a central Tuscan porch below a Venetian window, and a stucco finish.

For nearly 100 years, Cleave was the residence of one branch of the Snow family. Their ancestors were mayors, MPs and bankers in Exeter. Now there were Snows at Franklyn, at Cleave, in the Quarries, at Weircliff and at Whitestone House. At Christmas the Snow charity provided every Exwick child with a bright new sixpence and an orange.

At the beginning of this century, some of the employees of the Cleave estate lived in thatched cottages each side of the drive — 2 on the left, 5 on the right. The infants' Sunday School treat was held in the big house. The infants were collected in a horse-drawn mill-wagon. Since 1950 Cleve House has been owned by the Guide Dogs for the Blind Association. It is one of seven regional training centres. Additional bedrooms and kennels were built at the side and behind the main house. On 5th May 1988 Princess Alexandra re-opened the Centre after major renovations and extensions.

Exwick Cemetery (8 on map) was opened at Landhayes in 1877. Bishop Temple consecrated two identical chapels, to cater for non-conformists and church-goers, then led a procession over the burial-ground, reciting the 49th Psalm. The first interment was given a free tombstone. The melancholy inscription records that Elizabeth Curry, dying at 29, was joined a year later by her small son, and in 1880 by her young husband. A nearby stone was erected in memory of Robert Hodges "by the son of his wife, James Blackmore of Kobie, Japan." The path was bordered with yews and firs, but the yews were rooted out after a stray bullock ate a twig and died. In World War II a landmine exploded and threw a tall tree across the main road. The Cemetery has been extended several times, taking in hillside fields named Higher Barnclose, Lower Barnclose, Long Meadow, Water Park and Wheatley.

Treetops is a single-storey Day Centre for adults with multiple handicaps, where they can enjoy each other's company and a variety of activities in a pleasant setting.

For centuries, Foxhayes was a tiny hamlet with only two landmarks: the entrance to Cleave Drive, and the farmhouse opposite. Exwick Road zig-zagged in front of the farmhouse. Cleave Drive has become Winchester Avenue, leading to houses built over the higher fields of the farm, on roads named after other cathedral cities. The farmhouse was converted in 1937 into a pub, *The Thatched House*. The former farmer's name is preserved in Guy's Road. Simey Close commemorates a long-serving chairman of Exeter Housing Society. Foxhayes School in Gloucester Road opened in 1971, the first school to be specifically designed for modern teaching methods.

Ennerdale Way leads to Exwick Playing Fields. In 1980, once the flood relief work was finished, three football pitches and a cricket pitch were laid out. Changing rooms with accommodation for a warden were built in 1983, and some very solid vandal-proof toilets.

In 1981 the bakery extended over Valley Road. New Valley Road is part of a planned relief road. The local GPs built a Health Centre here in 1985. The aroma of fresh-baked bread wafts over the river-meadows — a reminder that flour was milled on these banks for over a thousand years, and that the monks of St Andrew's baked loaves to give to the poor — aptly enough, since it was Andrew who noticed the boy with the five barley loaves, enabling Jesus to feed five thousand at the waterside.

Exwick Playing Fields

Acknowledgements

The area was *terra incognita* to the author. This booklet is therefore a monument to the kindness of those who provided information and reminiscences. Harold and Rhona Ackland let me pillage their scrapbooks and memories, Kenneth Ashton lent his file of research on *The Hermitage*. A member of the Civic Society lent her memoirs. Mrs. V. J. H. Gregory, Mr. Gardiner, K. D. Hornsby, Lawrence Taylor and the retired superintendant of Exwick cemetery provided interesting details. Further help came from Michael Dickinson, John Fairweather, Aileen Fox, John Havill, Richard Parker, Michael Smith, Mark Stoyle, Berhnese Woodman and Michael Woollacott. Much material lay in the Westcountry Studies Library, (especially the cuttings files), the Devon and Exeter Institution, the Friends' Library in Euston Road, and the Devon Record Office. Mrs. Parker kindly gave permission to use the map from the Buller Estate papers. The British Library gave permission to use the 1801 Ordnance Survey. I will deposit a fuller list of sources in the W.S.L.

P. V. Pitman kindly provided her drawings of now-vanished scenes: the originals are in the R.A.M. Museum. The Sclater family lent photographs of their nurseries. Edwin Crook lent the "Last Tram" postcard.

Thanks also to Rodney Fry for the route-maps, John Saunders for photographic work, Sheila Venn and Frank Harvey for typing, and Gilbert Venn for expert help with the lay-out and pasting-up.

Generous grants towards production costs were given by Exeter City Council, the Iverdean Trust and the Devon Northcott Foundation.

Hazel Harvey

Published by Exeter Civic Society.

Hon. Admin. Secretary: Mrs. J. Kumik,
7 Glasshouse Lane, Exeter.

Typeset by Owen Pook, Exeter.

ISBN 0 9505873 3 8

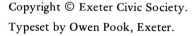

Remains of ancient Cross against wall, Cowick Str near Barton Road.